★

FROM
VENICE
TO
ISTANBUL

★

RICK STEIN
FROM VENICE TO ISTANBUL

BBC BOOKS

This book is dedicated to Ed, Jack and Charlie and Sas, Zach and Olive

10 9 8 7 6 5 4 3 2 1

BBC Books, an imprint of Ebury Publishing
20 Vauxhall Bridge Road
London SW1V 2SA

BBC Books is part of the Penguin Random House group of companies
whose addresses can be found at global.penguinrandomhouse.com

Penguin
Random House
UK

This book is published to accompany the television series entitled
Rick Stein: From Venice to Istanbul first broadcast on BBC Two in 2015.
Rick Stein: From Venice to Istanbul is a Denhams production.

Producer and director: David Pritchard
Associate producer: Arezoo Farahzad
Executive producer for the BBC: Lindsay Bradbury

First published by BBC Books in 2015

www.eburypublishing.co.uk

A CIP catalogue record for this book is available from the British Library

ISBN 9781849908603

Printed and bound by Firmengruppe, Appl, aprinta druck,
Wemding, Germany

Penguin Random House is committed to a sustainable future for
our business, our readers and our planet. This book is made from
Forest Stewardship Council® certified paper.

Commissioning editor: Lizzy Gray
Project editor: Mari Roberts
Editor: Charlotte Macdonald
Design and art direction: Smith & Gilmour
Photographer: James Murphy
Food stylist: Aya Nishimura
Assistant food stylist: Xenia von Oswald
Prop stylist: Penny Markham

The publishers would like to thank Rüstem Pasha Mosque
for their kind assistance in the preparation of this book.

INTRODUCTION

To fit in with work at the restaurant I write my recipes in the morning. I start at ten thirty and the thought of lunch becomes a growing pleasure as I get hungrier. It's around then that my heart turns fondly to thoughts of the Eastern Mediterranean, the olive oil, the tomatoes, the red onions, the wild oregano, the lemons, the sweet fish, the lean lamb, the wine, the olives, the capers and the garlic. It turns, too, to potatoes so waxy that frying them in wedges in olive oil makes the best chips in the world. I forget the richly spiced dishes of my last journey to India and I think instead of the lightly aromatic quality of a simple fish stew of John Dory and rascasse from Pylos in Greece, made just with onions, garlic, white wine, potatoes and lots of olive oil. I sat down with my friends at the restaurant there, having ordered a Greek salad and some bread, which clearly came from the bakery in the square, and a bottle of white wine that was a blend of Chardonnay and Gewürztraminer. It was lovely. Up to then, I had been ordering retsina, but somehow its scent of pine resin didn't carry the same shock of strangeness as it did in the 1970s. In those days, there was nothing else other than a white called Domestica, which had the same effect on serotonin levels as a British beer called Whitbread Tankard – you drank it, but felt there had to be a better way. The Greek salad had changed for the better, too. There was a whole slab of feta on top of the peeled cucumbers, tomatoes, onions and olives, which had been sprinkled with oregano. The olive oil and vinegar came in separate bottles: profligate with the oil and miserly with the vinegar is my take on a dressing, then salt and black pepper, and break up that gorgeous crumbly feta into the salad.

The fish stew was nothing remarkable but the potatoes were warm and earthy, the fish straight out of the bay, the bread still warm, the wine cool, tart and aromatic. That night we went filming in a hillside village called Messochori. Its restaurant, Trixordo, is famous for rebetiko: urban poor people's music, like the blues, about the harsh realities of living under the radar. Music as the anthropologist Elias Petropoulos said, of 'the jail and the hash den'; songs of *meraki*, *kefi* and *kaimos* – love, joy and sorrow – like the dance in the film *Zorba the Greek*. 'When Zorba dances, you dance' it said on the poster of the film when it was released in the 1960s. I read the book, by Nikos Kazantzakis, on a long sunny voyage in a caique to the island of Kalymnos. I remember the continual presence of death in the novel, but also the sun, the serenity, the wine-dark sea, the white houses and, as we sailed, the thrill of blue distant islands, hills of goats and olive groves, limestone rocks and beaches all around and the scent of mountain herbs on the breeze. The book combined the darkness of death with a joy, too, in Zorba's affirmation of life. You might as well dance, it said to me.

That night the spirited rebetiko dancers promised to us by the restaurant owner, our fixer, Mr Karalis, failed to show up. It turned out they had already started the summer season working in the beach bars of Kavos on Corfu. Mr Karalis prepared a lamb and potato stew with olive oil and lemon in the wood-fired oven in the garden. It was plain he didn't do it very often, but his lamb turned out deliciously lemony and salty. At the same time the cook at the restaurant made a pile of pancakes, each one sprinkled with grated mizithra cheese, pungent and salty. That's going to be tasteless, I thought, but it wasn't. I was almost looking for things not to be good, only to be proved wrong each time.

There was one rebetiko dancer who didn't exactly look as though he possessed a fiery soul like an artist of flamenco, which rebetiko so resembles. The musicians, playing bouzouki, guitar and baglamas, all looked like music teachers, but they entered into the spirit of the thing and the dancer clearly knew the dance. A few English and Germans got up and I joined in. We all started holding hands and swaying, kicking our feet and clicking our fingers, with me thinking about the shared humanity of flamenco, blues or rebetiko, and how a rubbish dancer like me can suddenly dance if the music is that soulful.

'How can we know the dancer from the dance?' wrote Yeats. It was thoughts from another Yeats poem, 'Sailing to Byzantium', that accompanied me on this culinary journey from Venice to Croatia, Albania, Greece and Turkey. Byzantium, as Istanbul was known in ancient times, represented to him the artistic imagination; he thought of it as a place of fabulous colour and brightness. The thought of finishing in Istanbul filled me, too, with a sense of ending in one of the world's great cities, where the food in its opulent complexity would match the images of golden mosaics, and a fabulous former cathedral, Hagia Sophia, would put 'The fury and the mire of human veins' into perspective.

Even in Venice the shapes and colours of Byzantine art and architecture pointed the way. A lunch at Locanda Cipriani on the island of Torcello in the lagoon necessitated a return to the Cathedral of Santa Maria Assunta, there to gaze at the sublime mosaic of the Virgin and Child, her expression one of mystic piety as she points with her delicate long fingers to the infant Christ as the source of the salvation of mankind. The gold background, the towering figure in blue and the infant with the face of someone much older are like a portal into a different world, one that is echoed to me by the food from this part of the world. So often in Turkey I kept thinking of how the flavours were as if from a parallel universe: the sharpness of yogurt, common in so many dishes, and its affinity with lamb; the lemony favour of sumac; the spiciness of red pepper paste; the plethora of fruit, nuts and cinnamon in rice dishes; the fondness for aniseed-flavoured drinks and smoky aubergines. The acidic and salty cheeses from sheep and goat's milk, some matured in goat skins. Salads made from boiled wheat, grains flavoured with pomegranate molasses, pies made with crisp filo pastry filled with the same tart cheese and wild greens gathered from the hillsides. The hot menthol flavour of wild oregano. A flatbread sandwich of cold lamb's brains, red onion, tomato, parsley and chilli flakes, sold with a sour drink, şalgam, of fermented and salted purple carrot juice. I often found myself struggling to take in the many new and strange flavours thrust on me, tastes that would eventually fill my memory with nostalgia.

I like to think of the cities of Venice and Istanbul as two large books propping up a shelf full of stories about the cooking of the Eastern Mediterranean. Tales like a Greek pie maker and her daughter in a Zagorian village in the Pindus mountains north of Ioannina, whose chicken pie caused me to shake their hands in earnest congratulation; or a pilgrimage to the Mani in the Peloponnese to visit the house of the late travel writer Patrick Leigh Fermor and discover a recipe for moussaka, which he claimed not to like; or the morning spent high above the city of Split in Croatia with eyes streaming, watching the cooking of a whole sheep on a spit over a wood fire in a smoke-filled room. And earlier the goriness of a room below filled with hanging lambs slaughtered and waiting for impalement, then the roasting and the somewhat guilty delight in the moistness and tenderness of the slow-cooked meat.

It wasn't hard to find Eastern influences in the cooking of Venice either, whose wealth came from the Byzantine Empire and beyond. Venetian dishes are surprisingly uncomplicated for a city with such a rich history. It is primarily the produce of the lagoon and the Adriatic, and the almost waterlogged land that surrounds the city. But it is the seafood that fills my imagination whenever I go there: tiny shrimps fried in their shells in olive oil and scattered over soft polenta; the meat of the spider crab in a seafood-flavoured sauce tossed with freshly made potato gnocchi; the Rialto market just by the Grand Canal with piles of tiny soles, bass, octopus and sardines split open ready for frying – perhaps the most colourful fish market in the world but sadly getting inextricably smaller as residents leave the city and tourism increases.

It's a problem, but so is the sinking of the city and the rising of sea levels. So is the reality of a couple of nice elderly English tourists on a vaporetto complaining they'd been charged 34 euros each for lasagne. It's much the same in Greece where we learnt how moussaka is often made in vast trays in Romania, frozen and sawn into portions for the tourist market. Yet it doesn't stop you finding a moussaka cooked in a little house in Kardamyli in the Peloponnese where each ingredient, including long slices of potato, is fried before being layered with béchamel and tomato sauce and baked to complete perfection. Nor does it stop me being taken by Francesco da Mosto to a tiny restaurant called Antiche Carampane in San Polo, the historic courtesans' area of Venice, there to eat bigoli in cassopipa, a thick spaghetti-shaped pasta with a shellfish sauce, made by cooking the shellfish in a pot with leeks, carrot, onion and a spice mix that could only have come from the East, containing nutmeg, cardamom, cinnamon and cloves. In the menu case outside it says:

No Pizza
No Lasagne
No Menu Turistico

Thoughts of Byzantine culture followed me across the Adriatic to Croatia. We had stopped off at Ravenna on the way to the port of Ancona to see the mosaic there of the Eastern Roman emperor Justinian I and the empress Theodora, who built Hagia Sophia in Constantinople, and found time to enjoy a real ragù bolognese and take in the local flatbread stuffed with cheese, prosciutto and tomato: the piadina.

In Croatia there were plenty of Byzantine churches to continue the sense of edging towards the Eastern end of the Christian Roman Empire. I enjoy the shape of Byzantine churches, their proportions, the satisfying, almost human quality to the arches and domes, coupled with the dark, warm interiors and scents of incense and candle smoke. There's a powerful connection for me between that and the flavours of the Dalmatian coast, the goat's cheeses, the spit-roasted lamb eaten after a journey into the hills above Split to a Roman amphitheatre built for games by the emperor Diocletian right at the start of the Byzantine Empire. Venetian food followed us, too, right down to Albania - hardly surprising when one remembers that for almost

four hundred years the coast was part of the republic of Venice. For me, Croatia was a country of tall, beautiful women with high cheekbones, and a sense of Ruritania about the red, white and blue flag with its romantic coat of arms in the centre. However, I didn't miss the sense of a civil war recently fought, particularly when standing on the battlements in Dubrovnik looking up to the heights above, having learnt of the Serbian artillery raining shells down on to such a beautiful city. As in other countries with a history of recent civil war that I've travelled to – Cambodia, Vietnam, Spain – you can be fooled into thinking everyone wants to forget about it. The reality is only the very young can, but there's always a sense, too, in which enjoyment of food can be a way to forget. That's why I believe in celebrating and taking delight in eating good food. The French epicure Brillat-Savarin reminds us in one of my favourite books, *The Physiology of Taste*: 'The Pleasures of the table belong to all ages, to all conditions, to all countries and to every day; they can be associated with all the other pleasures and remain the last to console us for the loss of the rest.'

Such pleasures disappeared in Albania during the communist regime and following its collapse in 1990. The regime wiped out its culinary heritage; people forgot what they once had. Peasant agriculture, so important to countries like France, Italy, Spain and Greece, had been destroyed in favour of communal farming during the 45-year period of communist rule, and restaurants were non-existent. There is good food in Albania today but it is not vying for your attention as it does in Greece. The restaurants that opened soon after the regime fell were poor copies of Western fast food, but the situation is improving.

I went out fishing for prawns on a lagoon near the town of Lezhë in the north and the fisherman told me that during the communist era they fed prawns to pigs. We took those prawns back to a restaurant on a beach and they were cooked over charcoal in a lovely brick kitchen. The owners had arrived just as the communist regime was failing. They had brought along an old sofa to sit on under the trees by the water. They kept returning and cooking prawns and simple pilafs for their friends and gradually built up a restaurant, still cooking prawns, bass and mullet over an open fire, but now the guests were from all over Albania, especially the young men in dark suits and sunglasses driving brand new 4x4 Mercedes or Range Rovers with tinted windscreens, some of them right-hand drive. Where do they get the money for such magnificent vehicles? I kept thinking of Kipling's 'A Smuggler's Song': 'Watch the wall, my darling, while the Gentlemen go by.'

We sat by the water eating prawns and talking to our fixer, Blerina. In addition to speaking excellent English and being in regular contact on her mobile with a chum called Edi who, as prime minister, ran the country, she also looked like a young Audrey Hepburn. To us she represented a great future for the country: enthusiasm, a sense of humour, an awareness of things not right yet but a determination to make them better. In spite of the food shortages of the communist era, which her mother, who was also there with us, recalled, Blerina had childhood memories of the warm smell of tomatoes, cucumbers and olive oil at picnics on the beach at Vlorë. Cucumbers, tomatoes, onions, olive oil and sharp sheep's cheese and oregano – you get the same sort of salads whether you're in Albania, Croatia, Greece or Turkey. Add to that wonderful-tasting fish, lamb cooked over charcoal, meat stews with a big emphasis on the vegetables in them, pasta dishes not just in Italy but with minced meat, yogurt and spicy Aleppo pepper in Turkey, superb pilafs, wonderful pastries with honey and nuts, and everywhere olive oil and oregano.

MEZZE

Whether it's mezzes in Turkey or Greece, antipasti in Venice, or even tapas and pintxos in Spain, they are the best part of dinner.

I first went to Istanbul about twelve years ago. I stayed in Sultanahmet in a hotel next to the Blue Mosque, in a room so small I had to move my suitcase to get out of bed. But it didn't matter: the sheer atmosphere of the muezzin call to prayer at what was probably four o'clock every morning, the old wooden houses in the streets all around, the closeness of the Topkapı Palace, the Byzantine splendour of Hagia Sophia almost next door – all this was enough to fill me with thoughts of being in the most fabulous city in the world.

I discovered a small seafood restaurant called Balıkçı Sabahattin a couple of streets away and I am slightly ashamed to say that, but for a couple of balık ekmek sandwiches by the Galata Bridge over the Golden Horn and a glorious spiced pilaf with cinnamon and currants in a restaurant in the Grand Bazaar, I went to Balıkçı Sabahattin every night – and the reason? The great Black Sea fish such as bass, grouper, bonito and even turbot, and the mezzes.

I formed the opinion then, which hasn't changed since, whether it's mezzes in Turkey or Greece, antipasti in Venice, or even tapas and pintxos in Spain, they are the best part of dinner. No wonder everyone is putting small plates on restaurant menus everywhere these days. We all love a small plate of such things as hummus sprinkled with chickpeas and topped with hot chilli oil; deep-fried köfte of minced lamb and mint or of lentil and bulgur wheat with cumin and dill; or white anchovies with roasted beetroot and skordalia, a pile of strained yogurt with cucumber, garlic and mint; or a little salad of bulgur wheat with red onion, pomegranate molasses and hot red pepper. And my favourite, the wonderfully smoky aubergine purée called baba ghanoush. At Balıkçı Sabahattin there was all that *plus* grilled octopus with lemon and olive oil, barbecued sardines in vine leaves, mussels like they did in Albania with tomato and feta, tiny prawns fried in their shells, and some thinly sliced, lightly salted palamut (bonito) with red onion.

HUMMUS

I wasn't going to include a recipe for hummus. There are more than a couple around, and also I recalled filming a spectacular hummus in the town of Tarsus of St Paul fame in eastern Turkey. But when I searched for the recipe in my *Mediterranean Escapes* book, it wasn't there. I couldn't believe it. How could I have left it out? I couldn't remember exactly how it was made, so I typed it into my computer and up came the dish on YouTube with me talking about it. What I do remember is the way the hummus was made to order and served warm and finished with whole chickpeas and sizzling hot oil with chilli in it.

SERVES FOUR TO EIGHT

200g dried chickpeas
1½ tsp bicarbonate of soda
15g/3 cloves garlic,
    crushed or grated
5 tbsp tahini paste
1 lemon, juiced
½ tsp salt

For the topping
½ tbsp tahini paste
1 tsp sumac
1 tsp ground cumin
Small handful
    coriander leaves
2 tbsp olive oil
3g/1 small clove garlic,
    crushed or grated
1 tsp chilli flakes

Soak the dried chickpeas in plenty of water and 1 teaspoon of bicarbonate of soda, ideally for 24 hours. The following day, rinse and put in a pan with plenty more cold water and another ½ teaspoon of bicarbonate of soda. Bring the pan up to the boil, turn down to a simmer and cook until tender. This should take about 2 hours, but depending on the beans could take more or less. Top up the water if required. When really soft but not mushy, drain the chickpeas, reserving some of the water.

Put 2 tablespoons of the chickpeas aside and liquidize the remainder with the garlic, tahini, 1 tablespoon of lemon juice, salt and enough of the reserved cooking liquor to loosen the consistency.

Transfer to a serving bowl. Sprinkle with the rest of the lemon juice, drizzle with tahini, then scatter over the sumac, cumin and coriander leaves. Top with the reserved whole chickpeas.

In a small pan, heat the oil until very hot, then add the garlic and chilli flakes and stir briefly. Drizzle over the hummus and serve.

MUHAMMARA

The more you make muhammara, the more you will adjust the spices to your own liking. This is delicious as a dip, or spooned on top of chicken, grilled meats or fish. Muhammara will keep in an airtight container in the fridge for about a week.

2 red peppers, roasted and peeled, or use from a jar
175g walnuts, toasted
50g panko (or toasted white) breadcrumbs
2 tsp pomegranate molasses
10g/2 cloves garlic
2 tsp *Red pepper paste* (page 307)
2 tbsp lemon juice
1 tsp paprika
½ tsp ground cumin
1 tsp salt
6 turns black peppermill
4 tbsp olive oil

Combine the peppers and walnuts in a food processor and blend until smooth. Add the remaining ingredients except the olive oil and pulse until smooth. With the processor running, add the olive oil slowly and blend until the oil is completely incorporated. Turn off the processor and scrape down the sides of the bowl as you go. Serve at room temperature.

AVGOLEMONO SOUP

I had never seen this egg-thickened soup served with a poached egg, but it seemed like a good idea so I tried it – and it is. Like many a simple soup, its success depends on a really good stock. My chicken stock on page 307 fits the bill. Most of the time I've had this in Greece it's been made with rice, but the first time, years ago, it was with rice-shaped pasta, orzo. I thought it was a local giant rice, but avgolemono with orzo it always is for me now. I think the flour from the pasta imparts velvety smoothness. I whisk in a little butter at the end, too, to give an extra gloss. *Recipe photograph overleaf*

SERVES FOUR

8 eggs
1.5 litres *Chicken stock*
    (page 307)
1 tsp salt
1 skinless chicken breast,
    weighing about 170g
100g orzo pasta
3 tbsp lemon juice
30g butter
Small handful
    parsley, chopped
Cayenne pepper

Poach 4 of the eggs in simmering water for 3–4 minutes, then remove to a bowl of cold water to arrest the cooking. Refresh in hot water just before serving.

Heat the stock to a gentle simmer, add the salt, then poach the chicken breast for 20 minutes. Remove from the stock and allow to cool. Bring the stock to the boil, add the orzo pasta then reduce to a simmer and cook for 7–8 minutes. When the chicken breast is cool enough to handle, slice into 4 lengthways then cut across into strips and set aside.

Whisk the remaining 4 eggs with the lemon juice in a bowl. Pour half the hot stock over the egg/lemon mixture, whisking all the time, then put the egg, lemon and stock back into the pan, return to the heat and stir till the eggs thicken (at about 70–80°C). Don't cook any further.

Remove from the heat and whisk in the butter and parsley. Add the chicken strips to the soup and ladle into individual bowls. Add a reheated poached egg to each serving and sprinkle with a pinch of cayenne pepper.

RED LENTIL & BULGUR SOUP
Ezo gelin çorbası

When I first saw this soup on a menu in the hotel we were staying at in Çanakkale prior
to visiting Gallipoli, I was not filled with eagerness. But I learnt years ago in what were
then deeply foreign Chinese restaurants in Soho to choose the least appetizing dish
on the menu – boiled eel and black bean soup comes to mind – to be astonished.
So it was with Ezo gelin soup: a combination of lentils and rice. What I particularly
loved was the dried mint and the topping of hot butter and red chilli. Freshly
dried Turkish mint has an altogether different flavour to fresh.

SERVES FOUR TO SIX

3 tbsp olive oil
1 large onion, chopped
10g/2 cloves garlic,
   crushed or grated
2 tbsp sweet paprika
½ tsp chilli flakes
2 tbsp tomato paste
200ml passata
250g red lentils, rinsed
50g long-grain rice, rinsed
1.5 litres *Chicken stock*
   (page 307)
50g bulgur wheat, rinsed
1½ tbsp dried mint
1 tsp salt

For the topping
2 tbsp butter, melted
1 tsp sweet paprika
1 tsp dried mint
Pinch chilli flakes

In a large saucepan, heat the olive oil over a medium heat.
Add the onion and garlic and cook for about 5 minutes
until soft, then add the paprika and chilli flakes. Stir for
1–2 minutes before adding the tomato paste and passata.

Add the lentils, rice and chicken stock, bring to the
boil, then reduce to a simmer and cook for 25 minutes
until the lentils are very soft and pulpy.

Add the bulgur wheat and the dried mint and cook
for a further 10 minutes until the bulgur has softened.
Add the salt, then taste to check the seasoning and adjust
if necessary. Ladle into bowls and served drizzled with
a little of the melted butter into which you have stirred
the paprika, mint and chilli flakes.

RED LENTIL PATTIES
Mercimek köftesi

In Turkey we filmed, somewhat bizarrely at about four o'clock in the afternoon, what was explained to us as a typical Turkish breakfast, yet it wasn't out of kilter that it was still being served so late. It comprised twelve to fifteen dishes, including three or four cheeses, menemen (scrambled eggs with tomato and red peppers, see page 82), candied fruits, a Turkish version of Greek salad, breads, a couple of köfte-type dishes, cacık (yogurt with garlic, cucumber and mint, see page 35) and these red lentil patties, which are generally served cold. This is the sort of dish that makes the Turkish mezze so special.

SERVES FOUR TO EIGHT

100g red lentils, rinsed
500ml water
½ tsp salt
100g bulgur wheat, rinsed
3 tbsp olive oil
1 small onion, finely chopped
10g/2 cloves garlic, crushed
  or grated
1 tsp ground cumin
1½ tbsp tomato paste
1 tsp *Red pepper paste*
  (page 307)
4 spring onions, finely sliced
Small handful dill, chopped
Small handful flat-leaf
  parsley, chopped
Juice ½ lemon
Salt and freshly ground
  black pepper

To serve
Little Gem lettuce leaves
Wedges of lemon

Put the lentils, water and salt in a large pan with a lid and bring up to the boil. Turn down to a simmer and cook until most of the water is absorbed, 8–10 minutes. Add the bulgur wheat, turn off the heat, stir to mix and cover with a lid. Leave the bulgur wheat to absorb the remaining liquid for about 10 minutes.

Heat the olive oil in a separate pan over a medium heat and sauté the onion for about 5 minutes until softened, then add the garlic, cumin, and tomato and red pepper pastes.

When the bulgur wheat is ready, stir in the tomato and onion mixture together with the spring onions, chopped herbs and lemon juice, and season with salt and pepper. With damp hands, shape the mixture into elongated lemon shapes. Serve each one in a lettuce leaf, with lemon wedges on the side.

ROASTED BEETROOT WITH ALMOND SKORDALIA & WHITE ANCHOVIES

I have two recipes for skordalia in the book: a plain potato, olive oil and garlic one (page 308), and this one made with almonds, white wine vinegar and garlic. I am addicted to garlic sauces anyway – aïoli, alioli, and the delicious warm anchovy, garlic and olive oil sauce called bagna cauda from Italy – but this skordalia makes a lovely combination with the earthy taste of the beetroot and the sharpness of freshly pickled anchovies (see the marinated anchovies on page 65). Use mixed varieties of beetroot if you can get them. *Recipe photograph overleaf*

SERVES FOUR TO EIGHT

1kg fresh beetroot (4 large), peeled and quartered
2 tbsp olive oil
Salt and freshly ground black pepper
85–100g white anchovies
Small handful flat-leaf parsley, roughly chopped

For the skordalia
250g potatoes, peeled and quartered
5g/1 clove garlic, crushed or grated
25ml white wine vinegar
70ml olive oil
1 tsp salt
8 turns black peppermill
20g blanched almonds, finely chopped
2 tbsp water

Heat the oven to 200°C/gas 6. Drizzle the beetroot with the olive oil, sprinkle with salt and pepper and roast for 45–50 minutes until tender.

While the beetroots are roasting, make the skordalia by boiling the potatoes in salted water until tender. Drain well, then mash or rice the potatoes into a bowl. Add the garlic, then the vinegar and olive oil alternately, a spoonful at a time, beating after each addition. Stir in the salt, pepper and almonds. Loosen the consistency with the water.

Serve the skordalia topped with chunks of beetroot, a few anchovies and some chopped parsley.

BEETROOT DIP
Pancar ezmesi

I am always fascinated by the popularity of dill in Greece and Turkey because for me
it is the herb of Scandinavian cured fish – gravadlax/gravlax: salmon cured with sugar,
salt and dill – and yet it is extraordinarily good with yogurt, garlic and beetroot.
Dips like this and muhammara (page 20) are the perfect accompaniment
to freshly baked pide bread (page 32).

SERVES FOUR TO EIGHT

500g beetroot (3 medium
 or 2 large)
15g/3 cloves garlic,
 crushed or grated
250ml Greek-style yogurt
Small bunch dill, chopped
30ml olive oil
1 tsp salt
6 turns black peppermill

Put the beetroots in their skins in a saucepan, cover with
water and cook for 30 minutes or until tender. Drain and
allow to cool enough to handle, then slip their skins off.
In a food processor, blend the beetroot and garlic. Transfer
to a bowl and mix in the yogurt, dill, olive oil and salt
and pepper. Serve at room temperature.

PIDE BREAD

I can't resist pide, which is to Turkey what focaccia is to Italy. I first came across it on visits to Australia in the late 1980s and early 1990s. Then it was rather exotic, now it is everywhere, but I still favour the recipe that we use at The Seafood Restaurant, flavoured with garlic and rosemary.

SERVES FOUR TO SIX

10g dried active yeast
1 tsp sugar
450ml tepid tap water
700g white bread flour,
    plus extra for dusting
1½ tsp salt
10g unsalted butter
    or 1 tbsp olive oil
1 tbsp semolina or
    polenta, for dusting

For the topping
5g/1 clove garlic, bruised
    with the back of knife
    or rolling pin
50ml olive oil
1 sprig rosemary,
    leaves detached
1 tsp flaky sea salt

Combine the yeast, sugar and tepid water in a jug and leave in a warm place until it froths. In a large bowl, mix the flour and salt, rub in the butter or olive oil, then add the yeast mixture. Bring together into a dough and knead by hand for 10 minutes (or using a dough hook in a food mixer) until smooth and elastic. Place the ball of dough in an oiled bowl, cover with cling film and leave to rise for about an hour until doubled in bulk.

While the dough is rising, combine the garlic and olive oil in a pan and warm through, then turn off the heat and leave to infuse. When cooled, add the rosemary leaves and set aside.

Knock back the dough when ready on a floured surface and divide into two. Cover and leave to rest for a further 15 minutes.

Heat the oven to 240°C/gas 9, or as hot as it will go, and heat 2 baking trays or pizza stones.

Flatten the dough balls into large ovals with your hands or a rolling pin. Dust the baking trays or pizza stones with polenta or semolina, then place the dough on them. Make indentations with your fingers all over the surface of each and drizzle over the infused oil with rosemary. Sprinkle over the flaky salt. Bake for 10–12 minutes or until golden. Allow to cool a little, but eat while still warm.

STRAINED YOGURT WITH CUCUMBER, GARLIC, MINT & DILL

Cacık

Cacık is to Turkish cuisine what raita is to Indian. The enemy to great cacık is too much liquid, so use proper Greek yogurt, which has been strained, or strain your own by leaving in a fine sieve for an hour. For the same reason, it is important to peel and deseed the cucumber, grate it and salt it, and to squeeze it in kitchen paper to extract excess water.

SERVES FOUR TO EIGHT

2 cucumbers, peeled,
   deseeded and grated
1 tsp salt
500g Greek yogurt
1 tsp lemon juice
3g/1 small clove garlic,
   crushed or grated
1 tbsp chopped dill
Small handful mint
   leaves, chopped
½ tsp ground cumin
Salt and freshly ground
   black pepper
Pinch of cayenne pepper

Mix the grated cucumbers with the salt in a bowl. Set aside for 10 minutes to draw some of the liquid out of the cucumbers.

Drain the excess liquid from the bowl of cucumbers and squeeze them out between sheets of kitchen paper. Add to the yogurt in another bowl, then stir in the lemon juice, garlic, dill, mint and cumin. Mix well to combine. Adjust the seasoning as needed with salt and pepper. Sprinkle with cayenne before serving.

SMOKY AUBERGINE PURÉE WITH GARLIC, TAHINI & LEMON JUICE

Baba ghanoush

My method of grilling the aubergines ensures that the baba ghanoush has the correct amount of smoky flavour. Serve with pide (page 32) or flatbread (page 307).

SERVES FOUR TO EIGHT

1kg medium aubergines
15g/3 cloves garlic, crushed to a paste with a little salt
3 tbsp tahini paste
1 tbsp lemon juice
1 tsp olive oil, plus extra to serve
Salt
Seeds 1 pomegranate or small handful flat-leaf parsley, to garnish

Heat the grill to its highest setting and grill the aubergines for about 30 minutes, turning regularly until their skins are blackened, the insides feel soft and they smell smoky. This can also be done over charcoal on a barbecue.

Cut the aubergines in half lengthways and scoop out the soft flesh into a bowl. Using a potato masher, work into a coarse paste. Add the crushed garlic, tahini, lemon juice and olive oil and season with salt to taste. Mix well.

Transfer to a clean bowl and spread the purée out. Drizzle with a little more olive oil, garnish with pomegranate seeds or parsley and serve.

BAKED PUMPKIN WITH SUN-DRIED TOMATO PASTE & CRISPY ONIONS

Sinkonta

What a joy was Ayse Nur's garden. I remember a huge pile of golden orange pumpkins in front of an old blue door, which I thought said it all about autumn in Turkey. The whole garden was a harmonious retreat from the busy outside world into flowers, pomegranate and lemon trees. Ayse cooked this outside in her garden bread oven, and I must say it looked almost too easy. She said simply that this recipe from her aunt was the most popular dish in her restaurant, Asma Yaprağı in the centre of Alaçatı, and on tasting it I could understand why. Delicious even when made with ordinary tomato paste rather than the sun-dried paste she was using, called salça. *Recipe photograph overleaf*

SERVES FOUR TO EIGHT

1kg pumpkin, peeled, seeded and cut into chunky slices
3 medium onions, halved and sliced
1½ tsp fine salt
6 tbsp sun-dried tomato paste
12 turns black peppermill
2 tbsp plain flour
150ml olive oil, plus extra for greasing

Heat the oven to 200°C/gas 6. Grease the base of a roasting tin or ovenproof dish and arrange the pumpkin slices in it.

In a large bowl, mix the sliced onions with the salt. Massage the salt into the onions using your hands, to break them down a little. Mix in the tomato paste, black pepper and flour, then scatter all over the pumpkin. Drizzle the olive oil over the whole lot and bake for 30–40 minutes until the onions are starting to brown and the pumpkin is tender. Serve hot or warm.

KISIR

Salads like this and the freekeh salad on page 311 are what really excite me about Turkish food. I should also add the chickpea salad the director David Pritchard gave me on the following page. Every time I go to Turkey the food is so vigorous, yet so different to most European cooking, that it is almost like being in a parallel universe. This feeling is enhanced for me by visits to the fish markets and the restaurants on the Bosphorus in Istanbul, where they have fish such as Dover sole and turbot, not from our waters but from the Black Sea.

SERVES FOUR TO EIGHT

250ml boiling water
2 tbsp tomato paste
2 tsp *Red pepper paste*
   (page 307) or harissa,
   or 1 tsp smoked paprika
   (pimentón picante)
1 tsp salt
200g bulgur wheat, rinsed
1 tsp ground cumin
6 turns black peppermill
Handful mint, chopped
60ml olive oil
2 tbsp pomegranate molasses
Juice ½ lemon
1 small red onion, halved
   and finely sliced
2 tomatoes, deseeded
   and finely chopped
1 each green and red
   pepper, deseeded
   and finely chopped
5 spring onions, finely sliced
1 cucumber, halved, deseeded
   and finely chopped
1 bunch flat-leaf
   parsley, chopped
Lettuce leaves, such as Little
   Gem, to serve (optional)

In a jug, mix the boiling water with the tomato paste, red pepper paste (or harissa, etc.) and salt. Put the bulgur wheat in a bowl and pour over the water and tomato mixture, stir and leave to stand for 10 minutes covered in cling film until the liquid has been absorbed.

Fluff the bulgur up with a fork. Add the cumin, black pepper, mint, olive oil, pomegranate molasses, lemon juice and red onion and stir through well. Then lightly mix in the tomatoes, peppers, spring onions, cucumber and parsley. Serve at room temperature, in lettuce leaves if desired.

DAVID'S SALAD OF CHICKPEAS, CORIANDER, TOMATO & RED ONION

When David Pritchard, the television series director, gave me this recipe, I was a bit sceptical as to its Turkish origins as it contains coriander and fish sauce. The one herb you would expect to find all over Turkey is in fact very rare, although they do use it a little in eastern Turkey (see my recipe for hummus on page 18). As for Thai fish sauce, how could one justify it? About this time we were filming at Ephesus, the ruined Greek city on the Mediterranean near Izmir, and saw a kitchen with two original, very faded friezes, one of a pheasant, the other a red mullet. I then discovered that Ephesus was famous for garum, the Roman version of nam pla, and the most esteemed garum was made from red mullet. If being very purist, use salted anchovies, finely chopped, instead.

SERVES FOUR TO EIGHT

400g can or jar
   chickpeas, drained
1 medium red onion, sliced
2 medium tomatoes, chopped
1 red chilli, deseeded
   and chopped
Large handful coriander,
   roughly chopped
Juice ½ lemon
2 tsp Thai fish sauce
   (nam pla), or 2 salted
   anchovies, finely chopped
8g/1 large clove garlic, grated
45ml olive oil
½ tsp salt
6 turns black peppermill

Mix all the ingredients together in a bowl, tossing lightly. Serve.

SHALLOT STIFADO

This recipe comes from Neraida restaurant in Neapolis near Monemvasia in the Peloponnese. The chef, Pandelis Meimetis, explained that this must be made with the famous local onion, vatikiotika, which is exceptionally sweet and mild; shallots are a good substitute. The secret here is very long, slow cooking. As Pandelis says, the onions are so good his guests can't believe there is no meat in the recipe.

SERVES FOUR TO EIGHT

100ml olive oil
200g onions, chopped
20 shallots, peeled
   but left whole
1 tsp salt
12 turns black peppermill
1 tsp ground cumin
2 bay leaves
400ml passata
1 tbsp tomato paste

Heat the olive oil in a large pan over a medium heat and soften the chopped onions for 5 minutes before adding the whole shallots. Bring to the boil then reduce to a simmer and cook for 15 minutes. Then add the remaining ingredients and simmer for 1 hour. Allow to cool to room temperature before serving.

GIGANTES WITH TOMATOES & GREENS

I have to confess that when we were filming in Epirus in northern Greece, I had a couple of moments of severe doubt about the cooking. It is fabulous, wild, mountainous country, far from the southern sunny islands such as Mykonos or Ios. The river trout were good, though, as were the souvlakia or meat skewers, especially the marinated ones from the city of Metsovo near Ionannina where we were based. They also make great pies in the villages and grow plenty of giant butter beans, which they cook with tomatoes and wild greens (*horta*; see the horta pie on page 254). To make it easy, I have used chard here, in case you don't fancy going out to gather dandelions or sea kale.

Recipe photograph overleaf

SERVES FOUR TO EIGHT

500g dried gigantes beans (or butter beans if unavailable)
1 onion, chopped
10g/2 cloves garlic, chopped
6 tbsp olive oil
½ tsp sweet paprika
1 tbsp tomato paste
400g tin chopped tomatoes
100ml water
1 tsp salt
12 turns black peppermill
350g chard or spinach, washed
Small handful parsley, chopped
Small handful mint, chopped

Soak the beans overnight in plenty of cold water. Drain, rinse, cover with fresh water and bring to the boil, then turn down to a simmer and cook for 1½–2 hours until the beans are just tender.

Gently soften the onion and garlic in 2 tablespoons of the olive oil for 5 minutes. When soft, stir in the paprika, tomato paste and chopped tomatoes, water, salt and pepper. Bring to the boil then reduce to a simmer and cook for 30 minutes. Stir in the chard or spinach and take off the heat.

When the beans are cooked, drain them and mix with the tomato and spinach sauce, adding a further 2 tablespoons of olive oil and the chopped herbs.

Heat the oven to 160°C/gas 3. Transfer the beans to a casserole pan, drizzle with the last 2 tablespoons of olive oil and bake for 35–40 minutes until the beans are tender and the sauce thickened and bubbling. Serve hot, warm or at room temperature.

VEAL, MINT & OREGANO MEATBALLS IN A RICH TOMATO SAUCE
Keftedes

Don't we all love meatballs? This recipe comes from a taverna that was part of a farmhouse near Pylos by the bay of Navarino, run by Nakos, Saini, and Saini's wife Georgia who did the cooking for the taverna. While the kitchen was being set up for filming, I wandered through the farm and was accosted by an angry dog who barked ferociously then came roaring up to me wagging his tail. A bit like Chalky but bigger and fiercer, though not really fierce. Beyond the kennel was a vegetable garden filled with ripe aubergines, tomatoes, courgettes and okra. I could feel a piece-to-camera coming on, in which I said I am a little bit jaundiced by the view through the windows of an elegant restaurant into a carefully manicured vegetable garden. This scruffy but delightful garden, full of ripeness, guarded by a dog whose bark was worse than its bite, is what country restaurants should be like.

SERVES FOUR TO EIGHT

500g minced veal (or beef)
150g coarse breadcrumbs
1 egg, beaten
Handful mint leaves, chopped
1 tsp dried oregano
1 onion, grated
10g/2 cloves garlic, crushed
  or grated
50ml olive oil, plus extra
  for frying
30ml white wine
1 tsp salt
12 turns black peppermill
Plain flour, for coating

For the tomato sauce
60ml olive oil
6 tomatoes, roughly chopped
1 tsp salt
12 turns black peppermill
1 cinnamon stick

In a large bowl, mix together the meat, breadcrumbs, egg, mint, oregano, onion, garlic, olive oil, white wine, salt and pepper. With your hands, roll into golfball-sized meatballs and flatten slightly. Dust lightly in flour and fry in olive oil over a medium heat for 3–4 minutes per side, turning frequently to cook evenly.

In a separate pan over a medium heat, warm the olive oil, then add the tomatoes, salt, pepper and cinnamon stick, and cook gently for 20 minutes to make a pulpy sauce. Add the meatballs to the sauce, reheat for 5 minutes and serve.

HALLOUMI SAGANAKI

This is *the* way to cook halloumi. It is very popular done on a barbecue as a vegetarian burger, but served like this, dusted in semolina, fried in olive oil and drizzled with warm honey, black sesame seeds and oregano, it is one of the best mezzes I know. If you can get kefalotiri cheese, try that; it is very special too. *Recipe photograph overleaf*

SERVES FOUR TO EIGHT

225g block halloumi
  or kefalotiri cheese
2–3 tbsp olive oil
1 small egg, beaten
3 tbsp fine semolina
2 tbsp clear honey
1 tsp black sesame seeds
1 tsp dried oregano
10 turns black peppermill

Cut the halloumi horizontally through the middle. Heat the olive oil in a non-stick frying pan. Dip the halloumi slices in the beaten egg then roll in the semolina. Fry on a medium heat for a couple of minutes on each side until golden brown.

In a separate small pan, warm the honey. Serve the halloumi cut into squares, drizzled with warm honey and sprinkled with sesame seeds, oregano and black pepper.

FRITTURA DI PARANZA

Paranza means a 'trawl' – in other words, a fry-up of all the local catch. Every Mediterranean country has a similar dish. What I particularly like about this one, which I had at the Excelsior hotel in Venice, was not only the impeccable freshness of everything, but the inclusion of some sticks of fried spaghetti, which made the dish look very pretty. I suggest fillets of red mullet or gurnard, or even Dover sole, along with mackerel fillets, squid rings, octopus tentacles, scallops and prawns.

SERVES FOUR TO EIGHT

1kg mixed seafood
Salt and freshly ground
    black pepper
300g plain flour
    or semolina
750ml sunflower oil,
    for frying
20 pieces spaghetti,
    broken in half
Flaky sea salt, to serve
1 large lemon,
    cut into wedges

Season the seafood with salt and pepper. Dredge with flour and shake off any excess.

Heat the oil over medium-high heat in a frying pan, or use a deep-fat fryer. Add the fish in batches and fry for 1–2 minutes until golden brown, turning gently to cook evenly. Using a slotted spoon, remove the fish to drain on kitchen paper. Deep-fry the spaghetti for 1 minute at 180°C.

Pile the fish and spaghetti in a jumbled mound on a serving plate. Serve piping hot, sprinkled with sea salt and with lemon wedges on the side.

PRAWNS ALLA BUSARA

Travelling down the Dalmatian coast, it becomes clear very quickly how much is owed to the cuisine of Venice. After all, the area was once part of the Venetian Republic. This makes it a little difficult to find local seafood dishes, but scampi alla busara is an exception; even the Venetians will point out that its origin is across the Adriatic. It's traditionally made with scampi. Langoustine would be closest, but large prawns work well. In this case don't even think about shelling them before cooking – the joy is in sucking the juices out of the shells.

SERVES FOUR TO EIGHT

100ml olive oil,
    plus extra to serve
15g/3 cloves garlic,
    finely chopped
3 shallots, finely chopped
1 tbsp tomato paste
2 large ripe tomatoes,
    peeled and chopped
Pinch chilli flakes
Pinch saffron strands
1 tsp salt
250ml white wine
100ml water
24 large raw prawns, whole
10 turns black peppermill
2 tbsp breadcrumbs
Small handful flat-leaf
    parsley, roughly chopped
Crusty bread, to serve

Pour about 70ml olive oil in a frying pan and set over medium-high heat. Add the garlic and shallots. When they are sizzling, stir in the tomato paste, chopped tomatoes, chilli flakes and saffron and ½ teaspoon of the salt. Cook for 5 minutes, stirring constantly to prevent the shallots and garlic burning, then add the wine and cook for a minute.

Add the water and remaining salt, bring to the boil, stir, then reduce the heat and let the sauce simmer and reduce for 20 minutes while you fry the prawns.

Pour 30ml (2 tablespoons) olive oil in another frying pan and set over a high heat. When the pan is really hot, fry the prawns for a minute, then remove from the heat.

With the sauce still bubbling, add the fried prawns and coat them well. Season with black pepper, and add a tablespoon of the breadcrumbs. Use more crumbs if the sauce is too thin. Cook for a further 2 minutes then turn off the heat. Drizzle over a little more olive oil. Sprinkle with parsley and serve immediately with crusty bread.

GARLIC SHRIMPS WITH SOFT POLENTA
Schie con polenta

In Venice they use tiny shrimps from the lagoon called *schie*, which are served whole.
When I make this I use Falmouth Bay shrimps, which are a little bigger, so I remove the
heads. One of the ways of serving whole shrimps, i.e. head and all, is to snip off the sharp
spiny proboscis, called the rostrum, between the eyes. Though a little fiddly, it's worthwhile.
I am happy to crunch the shells, but even for me that part is too uncomfortable. This is
a perfect hot antipasti; the garlic and chilli juices form just enough sauce.

SERVES EIGHT

For the shrimps
90ml olive oil
800g whole raw
    Falmouth Bay shrimps
½ tsp salt
6 turns black peppermill
10g/2 cloves garlic,
    finely chopped
⅛ tsp chilli flakes
Juice ½ lemon
Small bunch flat-leaf
    parsley, chopped

For the soft polenta
150ml milk
600ml water
1 tsp salt
150g polenta (cornmeal)
50g unsalted butter, cubed

To make the polenta, put the milk and water in a large pan
along with the salt and bring to the boil. Add the cornmeal
to the boiling liquid in a thin continuous stream, whisking
all the time to avoid lumps. Stir for 1–2 minutes until it
starts to thicken, then turn the heat down low and cook
for 35–40 minutes, stirring every few minutes to prevent it
from catching on the bottom of the pan. When it is ready,
it should start to come away from the sides of the pan.
Beat in the cubed butter. Keep warm for a couple of
minutes while you fry the prawns.

Heat the oil in a large frying pan, add the shrimps and
stir-fry for a couple of minutes. Add the salt and pepper,
garlic, chilli and lemon juice, and half the parsley.

Spoon the soft polenta into a warmed serving bowl and
top with the shrimps, spooning over a little of the garlicky
juices from the pan. Sprinkle with the remaining parsley
and bring to the table at once.

SCALLOPS & BROAD BEANS ON SOURDOUGH TOAST

Cicchetti are Venice's answer to tapas. I was thinking of doing a whole series of them based on a visit to a famous cicchetti/tramezzini bar in Venice called All'Arco. These bars are known as bàcari. Owing to the vagaries of filming – in other words, spending too long in the previous location – we arrived just as the bar was running out. So I have come up with just one, my homage to a great snack and memories for me of a trip to Venice with my late friend Bill Baker, a famous wine merchant. We spent one glorious morning with some cicchetti here, a tramezzino there, and a small beer or a glass of wine locally known as an ombra.

SERVES FOUR

250g freshly podded
    broad beans
    (1kg weight in pods)
4 tbsp olive oil, plus
    extra to serve
1 shallot, finely chopped
5g/1 clove garlic,
    finely chopped
50g pancetta,
    finely chopped
1–2 tbsp water
Salt and freshly ground
    black pepper
4 small slices
    sourdough bread
8 scallops
1 tbsp finely chopped
    flat-leaf parsley

Boil the broad beans for 2–3 minutes. Drain and remove the tough skins.

Heat 3 tablespoons of the olive oil in a pan and gently fry the shallot, garlic and pancetta for 3–5 minutes. When soft, add the bright green broad beans and the water, and cook for a couple of minutes. Lightly mash the beans with a potato masher or fork so you end up with a very rough purée, and season with ½ teaspoon of salt and pepper to taste.

Toast the bread. While it is toasting, set a frying pan over a high heat with the remaining olive oil and, when hot, add the scallops, sear for 2 minutes on each side and season with a little salt and pepper.

Drizzle each slice of toast with olive oil, top with a spoonful of the broad bean purée and 2 scallops per person. Finish with a little chopped parsley.

SALT COD, OLIVE OIL & GARLIC EMULSION

Baccalà mantecato

I owe Harry's Bar a great debt as not only is this dish based on one they serve there but so is the ravioli with sauteed mushrooms on page 251. Arrigo Cipriani says that you must use stockfish (dried cod) for making a baccalà but it is really hard to get, so I have used salt cod instead. It has a luxurious texture and taste, which also goes very well stirred through hot pasta with a little chopped parsley.

ENOUGH FOR ABOUT THIRTY CROSTINI

500g dried salt cod
500ml whole milk
3 whole black peppercorns
10g/2 cloves garlic
250ml olive oil
Freshly ground
   black pepper
Crostini (page 307)
Flat-leaf parsley,
   roughly chopped

The salt cod needs to be soaked for 24 hours in plenty of cold water.

Put the cod in a pan and pour over the milk. Add the peppercorns and garlic cloves and bring to the boil. Immediately turn down the heat to very low and poach gently for about 20 minutes. Lift the cod from the pan using a slotted spoon or fish slice and leave to cool slightly before handling. Remove the skin and any bones. Discard and strain the poaching milk and set aside, along with the garlic cloves.

In a food processor (or by hand using a pestle and mortar), mash the fish with about 3 tablespoons of the reserved milk and garlic cloves to give a stiff paste. Then, with the motor running, add the olive oil in a thin steady stream, as if making mayonnaise, to create a smooth and shiny paste. Season with black pepper. Spread on to crostini and sprinkle with roughly chopped parsley.

This paste could also be used as a pasta sauce: add a little more olive oil to loosen the mixture slightly and stir through hot pasta, then sprinkle with parsley.

TRAMEZZINI

I have suggested three fillings for tramezzini, the famous Venetian triangular sandwiches. Traditionally they were always made with cooked tuna, so I have done a recipe with tuna, boiled egg and mayonnaise. Then there is a version with prawns in a Marie Rose dressing with avocado, and finally one with layers of thinly sliced ham, pesto and mozzarella. The secret of good tramezzini is to get as much filling in as you dare, tamping down the edges. In Venice they bake a long tin loaf of bread that is particularly elastic, which they slice horizontally so they can make them in bulk. Our own supermarket white sliced bread is – unusually – just the right thing. *Recipe photograph overleaf*

MAKES SIX

12 slices (cheap) white bread
Mayonnaise

For filling 1
1 tin tuna, drained
1 tbsp mayonnaise
½ tsp salt
1 hard-boiled egg, sliced

For filling 2
2 tbsp mayonnaise
1 tsp tomato ketchup
100g cooked, shelled prawns
1 avocado, sliced

For filling 3
½ tbsp pesto
½ tbsp mayonnaise
100g wafer-thin sliced ham
1 ball mozzarella, sliced

The technique is to pile up lots of filling in the middle of one slice of the bread, leaving a border of 1.5cm around the edge. Top with the second slice, press down the edges and trim off the crusts. Cut in half on the diagonal.

First spread all the slices of bread thinly with mayonnaise, going right to the edges.

For filling number 1, combine the tuna with the mayo and salt. Pile on top of the sliced egg.

For filling 2, combine the mayo and ketchup and fold the prawns into it. Pile on top of the sliced avocado.

For filling 3, combine the pesto and mayo and spoon generously over the bread. Pile the ham and mozzarella on top.

Serve with cross-section fillings on display.

POLPETTE
SOLO CARNE BOVINA
TRAMEZZINO
TUTTO
DI NOSTRA
PRODUZIONE

FRIED SARDINES WITH PINE NUTS & SULTANAS

Sarde in saor

This is such a good dish when done well and so disappointing when it's not – even in Venice, if the sauce is too sharp. The secret is – inevitably – really fresh Mediterranean sardines and a careful balance of sweet and sour. It is well worth making with our own Cornish sardines (previously known as pilchards, but much nicer now with a new name!). The only change I would make is to fillet them, as they are larger than the Venetian variety. My way of eating sardines on the bone is to hold them by the head and tail and just nibble at the flesh. Then you can drop the cleaned bones with head and tail still intact on to a plate with casual dexterity.

ENOUGH FOR ABOUT THIRTY CROSTINI

500g small sardines
(or larger Cornish
ones – see introduction),
scaled and gutted
400g red onions, finely sliced
4 tbsp olive oil
1 tsp coriander seeds, ground
1 clove, ground
100ml red wine vinegar
50ml cold water
½ tsp salt
60g sultanas, soaked for
30 minutes in hot water
then drained
60g pine nuts
Plain flour, for coating
Crostini (page 307)

Rinse the sardines and pat dry. If you are unable to buy small sardines to eat whole, you may want to fillet them at this stage.

Gently fry the onions in half the olive oil. When soft, add the ground coriander and ground clove, and cook for a minute before adding the vinegar mixed with the water, the salt, and the soaked and drained sultanas. Remove from the heat and set aside to cool, then add the pine nuts.

Roll the sardines (or fillets) lightly in flour and then shallow-fry them in the remainder of the olive oil in batches, until they are golden brown, then remove them to kitchen paper to drain. When cool, arrange them in a dish, alternating a layer of sardines with a layer of onions, pine nuts and sultanas. Cover with cling film and leave to rest for at least 24 hours before serving as a topping for crostini.

THREE GREEK SEAFOOD MEZZES

I thought it would be nice to suggest three seafood mezzes to be served at the same time: one hot, one warm and one cold. There has to be octopus somewhere – where would Greek seafood be without it? It's hard to get it exactly as the Greeks do, as they generally sun-dry the octopus before grilling it; you have probably noticed this around many a Greek harbourside. If not drying them, they will simmer them in lightly salted water for 50 minutes, drain and sprinkle with olive oil and oregano, then grill over charcoal and sprinkle with lemon and salt. You don't need to serve this hot but it mustn't be cold either. Like so much Greek food, tepid is the word. The anchovies you can make up beforehand. For me, it's the freshness of the anchovies and the simplicity of the preparation that count. The third dish is the tarama fritters on page 68. *Recipe photograph overleaf*

SERVES FOUR TO EIGHT

750g octopus, cleaned
3 tbsp olive oil, plus
    extra for brushing
Juice 1 lemon
1 tsp dried oregano
Salt

LIMENI-STYLE GRILLED OCTOPUS WITH LEMON JUICE, OREGANO & OLIVE OIL
Simmer the octopus in salted water for about 50 minutes until tender, then drain. When cool enough to handle, cut the tentacles into individual legs and the head into strips.

Brush with a little olive oil before grilling on a barbecue or under a hot grill for 3–5 minutes, turning regularly. The octopus should be nicely browned on the tips. Cut into 3–4cm chunks. Dress with the olive oil, lemon juice, oregano and some salt.

200ml freshly squeezed
    lemon juice
60ml olive oil
1 tsp chilli flakes
10g/2 cloves garlic,
    finely chopped
1 tsp dried oregano
Sea salt and freshly
    ground black pepper
500g whole fresh white
    anchovies, cleaned
    and filleted

MARINATED ANCHOVIES
In a shallow bowl, mix the lemon juice, oil, chilli flakes, garlic, oregano and some salt and pepper. Add the filleted anchovies and cover the bowl. Allow the fish to marinate for 30 minutes. Keeps for up to a week.

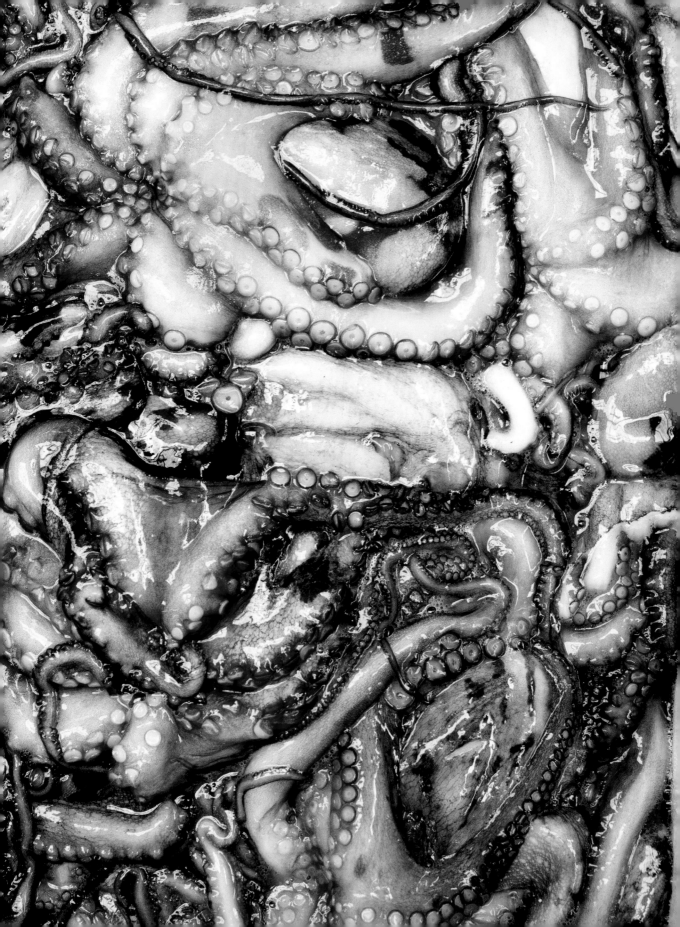

TARAMA FRITTERS

Vefa's Kitchen is to Greek cooking what *The Silver Spoon* is to Italian, Constance Spry to English and Stephanie Alexander to Australian. Not only does it cover food from all over Greece, but also wherever Greece has had an influence, particularly western Turkey. It means a lot to me, not just for lovely recipes like these tarama fritters – smoked cod's roe with garlic, mint and fresh breadcrumbs – but also because when I was on holiday in Puglia with my wife Sas and stepchildren Zach and Olivia at a converted *convento* run by Athena and the late Alistair McAlpine, they proffered the book and asked, 'Have you ever thought about producing a book on Greek food? It's really rather good.' Alistair died last January. We all miss him, so knowledgeable and enthusiastic about food was he, whether Italian, English or Greek. If it wasn't for him and Athena, I probably wouldn't have gone on this rambling journey from Venice to Istanbul. *Recipe photograph on previous page*

SERVES FOUR TO EIGHT

375g stale white bread,
    crusts removed
100g smoked cod's roe
8g/1½–2 cloves garlic, grated
½ onion, grated
2 tbsp finely chopped mint
2 tbsp finely chopped
    flat-leaf parsley
½ tsp dried oregano
    (optional)
Salt and freshly ground
    black pepper
Plain flour, for dusting and
    to add to mix if too wet
Vegetable oil, for frying
Cacık (page 35), to serve

Put the bread in a bowl, add water to cover and allow to soak for 30 minutes. Squeeze out the excess moisture with your hands, crumble the bread into another bowl and add the roe, garlic, onion and herbs and season with salt and pepper. Knead gently to combine.

Shape the mixture into 12–16 small balls, dust with flour and gently flatten into patties.

Heat the oil in a frying pan and fry the fritters over a high heat for 4–5 minutes on each side or until golden brown. Serve hot or at room temperature with cacık.

SHRIMP & DILL FRITTERS WITH OUZO

This comes from a tiny fishing village called Gerakas, forty minutes north of Monemvasia in the Peloponnese. The drive is spectacular, and Gerakas itself is the Greek fishing village by which all others must be judged. Like the shrimps with polenta (page 56), this was designed to use the tiny shrimps in the inlet on which Gerakas lies. I particularly enjoyed the subtle flavours of dill and ouzo.

SERVES FOUR TO EIGHT

175g plain flour
½ tsp baking powder
½ tsp salt
300ml water
1 tbsp ouzo (or pastis)
300g whole raw Falmouth
   Bay shrimps or brown
   shrimps, or 175g raw
   peeled prawns, cut
   into 5mm-thick slices
2 spring onions,
   very finely sliced
1 tbsp chopped dill
Olive oil, for shallow frying

In a large bowl, sift the flour and baking powder, add the salt, then make a well in the centre and add the water and ouzo. Gradually incorporate the flour into the liquid to make a thick batter. Fold in the prawns/shrimps, spring onions and dill.

Pour olive oil to a depth of about 5mm into a frying pan and place over a high heat. When hot, carefully add large spoonfuls of the batter into the pan and spread out a little with the back of a spoon so they develop thin, crispy edges. Cook 2–3 at a time, turn over after 2 minutes and repeat until puffed up and golden on both sides.

Remove from the pan and drain on kitchen paper. Serve immediately.

PRAWNS IN A SAUCE OF TOMATO, BASIL & FETA

This dish is often called prawn saganaki, which simply refers to the type of pan –
a small skillet – in which it is often cooked and served. In fact, serving seafood with
tomato and a cheese like feta is common throughout the Ionian region. This came from
the town of Preveza on the mainland of northern Greece, just opposite the island of
Lefkada. I had been promised a couple of dishes cooked by two fishermen's wives in the
local cooperative. When we got there, the cooking facilities in what appeared to be a
hostel were appealingly rudimentary. The building was indeed accommodation for the
local fishermen's cooperative, but it turned out they were there to guard a series of lagoons
where they trap migrating fish. Apparently theft of fish is rife in northern Greece,
particularly as a result of the recession, and I was disconcerted to find the ground littered
with used shotgun cartridges. I was also puzzled by the appearance of the two fishermen's
wives, one of whom was exceedingly glamorous in a green low-cut dress. I questioned my
esteemed director David afterwards, who admitted that what he had been promised
turned out to be two local dignitaries' wives who clearly wanted to be on TV.

SERVES FOUR TO EIGHT

200ml olive oil
1 leek, chopped
5 shallots, chopped
20g/4 cloves garlic, sliced
1kg whole raw prawns
100ml ouzo (or pastis)
4 tbsp tomato paste
100ml water
1 tsp salt
Handful flat-leaf
  parsley, chopped
250g feta cheese, crumbled
Large bunch basil
  leaves, chopped

Heat the olive oil in a large heavy pan over a medium heat
and sweat the leek, shallots and garlic for 5 minutes, then
add the prawns and cook for a minute. Pour in the ouzo,
cover with a lid and continue to cook for another minute.

Mix the tomato paste with the water and add this to the
pan before seasoning with the salt and adding the chopped
parsley. Stir and heat through, then add the feta cheese
and basil. Serve immediately.

OCTOPUS ALLA GLORIJET

I was very taken with the octopus recipe from the Glorijet restaurant near Dubrovnik. I find a lot of octopus dishes disappointing because octopus is not always as tasty as people think it should be. My two favourite ways of cooking are in the Greek style, charred over coals on a barbecue with lemon juice, olive oil and oregano (page 65), or simply boiled in salted water, as they do in Galicia, Spain, and sprinkled with pimentón picante (spicy smoked paprika) and olive oil. This octopus dish, however, really worked for me. It's just a simple tomato sauce with some new potatoes, capers and, surprisingly, samphire, but they have a lot of it in Croatia. The octopus is boiled, sliced and fried, then the sauce is added to it; it's not a stew. Very satisfying.

SERVES FOUR TO EIGHT

750g octopus, cleaned
Salt
Plain flour, for dusting
3 tbsp olive oil
4 tsp capers
120ml *Tomato sauce*
  (page 307)
300g new potatoes,
  halved and boiled
40ml white wine
Large handful samphire,
  boiled for 5 minutes
  then drained
1 green chilli, sliced,
  seeds left in
8 turns black peppermill

Simmer the octopus in salted water for about 50 minutes until tender, then drain. When cool enough to handle, cut the tentacles into individual legs and cut the head into long strips.

Cut the pieces into strips 3–4cm long and roll in flour. Heat the olive oil in a frying pan and fry the octopus pieces for 2 minutes, then add the capers, tomato sauce, cooked new potatoes, white wine, samphire, green chilli and black pepper, and warm everything through before serving.

PETROS'S CLAMS

Petros appears elsewhere as the owner of a bottarga factory in Messolonghi.
He invited us round to his father-in-law's house and cooked this clam dish for us.
I remember thinking at the time that he has put far too much lemon juice in it.
But Greece is the land of lemons and I think you simply get used to more of it,
particularly if used in a salty stock made from clam juice. The subtlety of this dish
lies in the shellfish stock he also added to the clams. I make this from any shellfish
scraps I have in the freezer; I often buy frozen North Atlantic prawns in the shell
to eat, and make stock from the heads and shells. *Recipe photograph overleaf*

SERVES FOUR

50ml olive oil
700g clams, in the
    shell, scrubbed
Small handful flat-leaf
    parsley, chopped
Juice and zest
    1 small lemon
½ tsp chilli flakes
½ tbsp roughly
    chopped oregano
Crusty bread, to serve

For the prawn stock
2 tbsp olive oil
3g/1 small clove garlic
250g shell-on prawns
    or heads and shells
1 tbsp tomato paste
½ tsp salt
300ml water

Make the prawn stock by heating the olive oil in a large
pan over a medium heat and adding the garlic and the
prawn heads and shells. Stir-fry for a couple of minutes
before adding the tomato paste, salt and water. Cook for
10 minutes, then pass through a sieve, pushing down on
the shells to extract as much of the prawn flavour as you
can. Discard the shells and set the stock aside.

In a large pan over a medium heat, warm the olive
oil and add the clams, parsley, lemon juice and chilli flakes
and cook for 2–3 minutes until the clams start to open.
Add 150ml of the prawn stock and cook for a further
2–3 minutes. Toss in the roughly chopped oregano
leaves, garnish with lemon zest and serve immediately,
with crusty bread to mop up the soupy juices.

★★ STREET FOOD

There is a something about the theatre of street food that is more powerful even than being in a buzzy restaurant.

To see a queue down a street somewhere in the Mediterranean with maybe steam rising or the scent of fried fish in the air – is there anything more exciting to those who love food? Waiting your turn outside a kiosk in Ravenna for a piadina filled with prosciutto and squacquerone, the local Taleggio-like cheese. Checking out a moustachioed, intimidatingly large, bald-headed menemen chef in the centre of Istanbul knocking out the gorgeous tomato, red pepper and green chilli scrambled-egg mess in two minutes flat. Trying to sit cross-legged while headscarfed ladies seated on the ground roll out dough for gözleme using a long rolling pin tapered at both ends and almost as thin as a drumstick, then pack with feta and spinach. Watching the world go by as I queue, again in Istanbul, for the ultimate offal takeaway: lamb's liver quickly fried with onions, chilli and garlic, sprinkled with sumac and cumin and wrapped in flatbread. Or köfte, be they from Adana or Gaziantep in Turkey or from Greece, with a splash of yogurt somewhere.

These are some of my favourite memories of Eastern Mediterranean cookery. To me the best thing about street food here is the accompaniment, particularly the pickles. Where would a lahmacun be without a few of those long, thin, pickled chillies common in Turkey and the Lebanon? Or the famous balık ekmek, grilled mackerel in a baguette: where would that be without the little plastic cup of pickled carrot, cauliflower and radish with coriander and chilli? There is a something about the theatre of street food that is more powerful even than being in a buzzy restaurant. In cities like London, New York, Sydney and Los Angeles, the more casual, the more pop-up a restaurant is, the more cutting-edge it seems, and it is all based on cooking in the streets. I bet if you have been to a place like Thailand with your kids, like I did years ago, and you ask them what they remember best, it will be something like eating crispy shrimp fritters with chilli sauce out of paper on the street.

THE TURKISH KING OF BREAKFASTS: EGGS WITH TOMATO, RED PEPPER & GREEN CHILLIES

Menemen

There are more recipes for menemen than you can shake a stick at, but I particularly like this one from a restaurant called Lades in Istanbul. The handsome, moustachioed chef, with a face for TV, clearly relished being filmed and did it so well. The egg had a particularly soft set and he served it in the pan he cooked it in. I have added a little feta on top, and I like to eat it with two or three pickled chillies too (see page 102). If you don't know how to pronounce the name, think of the *Muppets* song.

SERVES FOUR

50ml olive oil
½ small onion, thinly sliced
1 medium tomato, diced
½ red pepper, deseeded
   and diced
1 green finger chilli, halved
   lengthways and chopped
8 eggs, beaten
½ tsp salt
Freshly ground black pepper
60g feta cheese, crumbled

Heat the olive oil in a large frying pan over a medium heat. Add the onion and fry for 2–3 minutes to soften. Add the tomato, red pepper and chilli and cook for another 2 minutes.

Stir in the eggs. As the eggs cook, mix in the seasoning and the crumbled feta. Serve once you have a soft-set scrambled egg.

ÇILBIR

I sometimes think if you don't like yogurt you won't enjoy Turkish or indeed a lot of Greek cooking. To start with, the sourness of it is quite difficult but, once you get used to it, like so many special tastes, you become converted. I love this dish. I am going to put it on our café menu. The poached egg, the yogurt with a little salt and garlic, and melted butter with chilli flakes on top: just look at the picture and tell me you don't want to eat it.

SERVES FOUR

100g Greek-style
  yogurt, loosened with
  1 tablespoon of milk
5g/1 clove garlic,
  crushed or grated
½ tsp salt
4 eggs
Vinegar, for poaching
15g butter
½ tsp chilli flakes
Pide (page 32), to serve

Mix the yogurt, garlic and salt together and divide between 4 plates or bowls.

Poach the eggs in simmering water with a splash of vinegar for 3–4 minutes.

Melt the butter and add the chilli flakes.

Top each bowl of yogurt with a poached egg and drizzle over spicy butter. Serve with Turkish bread.

KAYIANA

This is a Greek version of menemen (see page 82), but it has smoked ham and a particular type of Greek loukaniko sausage made with fennel and orange. I couldn't find the sausage in London, or in Sydney for that matter, so I decided to make my own. It's not quite like the real thing but it has its own personality, which I think will charm you.

SERVES SIX

60ml olive oil
450g tomatoes, chopped
10 turns black peppermill,
   plus extra to serve
200g smoked ham,
   cut into 1cm cubes
200g *Loukaniko sausagemeat*
   (see facing page), formed
   into nutmeg-sized balls
12 eggs
1 tsp salt

Heat the oil in a large pan. Add the tomatoes and black pepper and simmer for 5 minutes.

In a non-stick frying pan, brown the smoked ham and sausagemeat balls over a medium-high heat, then lower the heat and cook for 10 minutes. Add the tomatoes to the frying pan.

Break the eggs into a bowl and beat, then add to the frying pan and stir gently to mix. Cook gently until you have a soft-set scrambled egg. Grind some more black pepper on top and serve.

LOUKANIKO SAUSAGEMEAT

You can use this mixture to form köfte on skewers or meat burgers or, of course,
make sausages with it. Makes enough for four kayiana recipes, ten to twelve
sausages or four to six burgers. It also freezes well.

MAKES ABOUT 900G

1 small leek
Olive oil
450g minced pork,
    preferably shoulder
150g minced lamb
250g minced pork fat
1½ tsp salt
18 turns black peppermill
15g/3 cloves garlic,
    crushed or grated
1 egg, beaten
1 tsp fennel seeds
1 tsp dried thyme
1 tsp dried oregano
1 tbsp red wine
Zest 1 orange
2 tbsp breadcrumbs

Finely chop the leek, sweat in 1 tablespoon of olive oil
over a medium heat until just soft, then set aside to cool.

Mix all the remaining ingredients with the leek and
2 tablespoons of olive oil, then chill in the fridge (to make
handling easier).

Form into sausages, burgers or, to make kayiana,
nutmeg-sized meatballs. Fry or grill the other shapes
as you would any sausages or burgers.

PIZZA BIANCO WITH SLICED POTATO, ONIONS, WHITE ANCHOVIES & TALEGGIO

I have only recently become enamoured with pizzas that don't contain tomato – actually at Passaparola, a famous pizza restaurant in Haberfield, Sydney. At the same time as not having tomato, it also had sliced potato, which seemed to me potentially quite bland. In fact, with a good cheese like Taleggio it was anything but, and now a 'white' pizza has become for me just as enjoyable as a Margherita. I am lucky enough to have an oven with a heated pizza stone in it. If you want the crispest possible base, I recommend you get hold of a pizza stone. It's better to pay good money for one, as cheap ones tend to crack.

MAKES FOUR LARGE PIZZAS

1 quantity *Flatbread dough*
    (page 307)
Olive oil, for greasing
Plain flour, for dusting

For the topping
2 waxy potatoes,
    sliced on a mandolin
120g Taleggio cheese
A few sprigs rosemary
    and/or oregano
Black olives and/or
    capers, optional
1 tsp flaky sea salt
Freshly ground black pepper
Olive oil, to drizzle
125g mozzarella ball, torn
30g pecorino romano, shaved
½ onion, very finely sliced
Anchovy fillets, to taste

Place the dough in a clean, lightly oiled bowl, cover with cling film and leave to rise for 30–60 minutes until doubled in size. Put 2 baking sheets or pizza stones into the oven and heat to 230°C/gas 8.

Blanch the potato slices in boiling salted water in a saucepan for 2 minutes. Drain well and set aside.

When ready, punch the dough down and knead again until smooth, then divide into 4. Roll each out with a rolling pin on a lightly floured surface into a rough circle about 25cm diameter and 3mm thick. Transfer 2 to the hot baking sheets/stones and top with half the quantity of Taleggio, potato slices, rosemary and/or oregano, and olives and/or capers if desired. Season with sea salt flakes and black pepper and drizzle over a little olive oil. Finish off with a little mozzarella and pecorino, sliced onions and fillets of white anchovy.

Bake for 7–10 minutes or until browned around the edges and bubbling. Serve immediately, then repeat with the other 2 pizzas.

KOKORETSI

I was in two minds about including this recipe in the book as many people are likely to find offal wrapped in intestines rather challenging. The original recipe calls for lamb's lungs, heart, liver and kidneys to be wrapped in intestines and cooked on a gently turning rotisserie over charcoal. I watched an expert cooking one in northern Greece. It needs a lot of skill: you have to slowly cook the intestines without overcooking the offal inside. I really liked it, but I think a slice is best eaten with other barbecued meats, such as souvlaki (see page 160), steak with a squeeze of lemon juice, or a pork chop. I have made the recipe much easier by using just liver and kidneys and wrapping them in caul fat, which is more tender and moist than intestines. I do think it's an excellent accompaniment to a mixed grill.

MAKES TWO TO THREE SKEWERS

300g lamb's liver,
    trimmed and cut
    into chunks
300g lamb's kidneys,
    trimmed and cut
    into chunks
Salt and freshly ground
    black pepper
1 tsp dried oregano
Caul fat
Olive oil, to drizzle
    and serve

Thread alternate chunks of liver and kidney on to 2 or 3 skewers about 25cm long. Season with salt, pepper and the oregano.

Wrap the whole skewer in caul fat and drizzle with olive oil. Grill over hot coals on a barbecue for 20–25 minutes.

Slide the meat off the skewers and cut into slices, sprinkle with a little more olive oil and seasoning, and serve.

PIADINA

Ravenna, just down the road from Venice, is the home of piadinas: flatbreads baked to order and filled with such delights as prosciutto, rocket and soft cheese. In Emilia-Romagna they serve them with a cheese called squacquerone. This is a local soft cheese that doesn't travel well, so for the rest of us it has to be Taleggio or mozzarella. Use the dough in the recipe below or, if you prefer a yeasted dough, use the flatbread recipe on page 307. *Recipe photograph overleaf*

MAKES EIGHT

For the dough
500g plain flour,
    plus extra for dusting
1 tsp fine sea salt
75ml olive oil
250ml warm water

*For the prosciutto filling
    (quantity per wrap)*
2 slices prosciutto
1 slice Taleggio cheese
Handful rocket
Olive oil, to drizzle
5 turns black peppermill

*For the chicken filling
    (quantity per wrap)*
¼ large cooked chicken breast
½ mozzarella ball, torn
Radicchio leaves, shredded
Olive oil, to drizzle
5 turns black peppermill

*For the anchovy and mayo
    filling (quantity per wrap)*
1 tbsp garlic mayonnaise,
    thinned with 1 tsp water,
    mixed with: ½ Little
    Gem lettuce, shredded:
    a few Parmesan cheese
    shavings; 1 brown
    anchovy fillet, chopped
1 medium tomato, sliced
5 turns black peppermill

Sift the flour into a large bowl and add the salt, olive oil and water. Stir to mix well into a rough, shaggy dough; if it is too dry to come together, add 1–2 tablespoons more water. Turn on to a lightly floured board (or into a food mixer with a dough hook) and knead for 5–10 minutes until smooth and elastic.

Prepare 8 fillings as desired, using the quantity given per wrap.

Divide the dough into 8 and roll into balls. Roll each one out into a circle 20–23cm across. Heat a non-stick frying pan on a high heat, add a circle of dough and cook for a minute or so until it bubbles and puffs up, then turn over and repeat on the other side. It will develop dark 'spots'. Wrap around fillings while warm and serve immediately.

PETOULES WITH MIZITHRA CHEESE

I watched these thin pancakes with salty mizithra cheese being cooked at a restaurant in the hills near Pylos. I thought the dish would be rather dull but it was utterly delicious. It was to be part of a night ending in a Zorba the Greek type dance called the rebetiko, the Greek version of flamenco. Unfortunately, the main dancers had already left the hills for summer jobs in Kavos on Corfu. The songs were good but I had to chip in with some dancing. The crew said I was 'quite' good.

SERVES FOUR

500ml water
1 tbsp salt
200g plain flour
½ onion
Olive oil
80g mizithra or pecorino
    romano cheese, grated

Put the water in a large bowl, add the salt and whisk in 1 tablespoon of flour at a time until you have a batter resembling pancake batter.

Drench the onion half in olive oil and rub around the base of a non-stick frying pan. Place over a medium heat and ladle in enough batter to cover the base thinly. Cook for about 2 minutes per side. Repeat until the batter is all used up. You should have about 8 pancakes.

Heat the oven to 180°C/gas 4. Stack the pancakes on a baking tray, sprinkling a layer of cheese between each one and finishing with cheese on top. Cook for 10 minutes until golden. Serve at once, cut into wedges.

GÖZLEME WITH FETA & SPINACH

Is there a more popular street food in Turkey than gözleme? They are as irresistible as a freshly cooked rumali roti in India, which, like gözleme, is cooked on an iron dome. These wafer-thin flatbreads are achieved by rolling each one out on a floured surface as thinly as possible. A filling is added to half of the disc, it is folded to form a crescent, then baked on the hot, slightly domed iron surface, brushed with butter and folded into a fan shape. Eating one straight away is heavenly. *Recipe photograph overleaf*

MAKES FOUR

⅔ quantity *Flatbread dough* (page 307)
Olive oil, for greasing and brushing
Plain flour, for dusting
Butter, to serve

For the filling
250g washed baby spinach
200g feta cheese, crumbled
4 spring onions, finely sliced
½ tsp chilli flakes

Alternative fillings
See *Lahmacun* (page 98) or 2 tbsp tahini and a drizzle of clear honey

Place the dough in a clean, lightly oiled bowl, cover with cling film and leave to rise for about 30 minutes to an hour until doubled in size.

Chop the baby spinach and mix in a bowl with the feta, spring onions and chilli flakes.

When ready, punch the dough down and knead again until smooth, then divide into 4 equal pieces. Roll each one out on a floured surface until you have a thin sheet just 2mm thick and about 25cm in diameter. Spread a quarter of the filling on to half of each sheet of dough, then fold over into a semi-circle. Brush one side of each gözleme with olive oil.

Heat a large non-stick frying pan or griddle. Cook each one for 2–3 minutes, then brush with olive oil, turn over and cook on the other side for another 2–3 minutes. Serve immediately, with butter melting over.

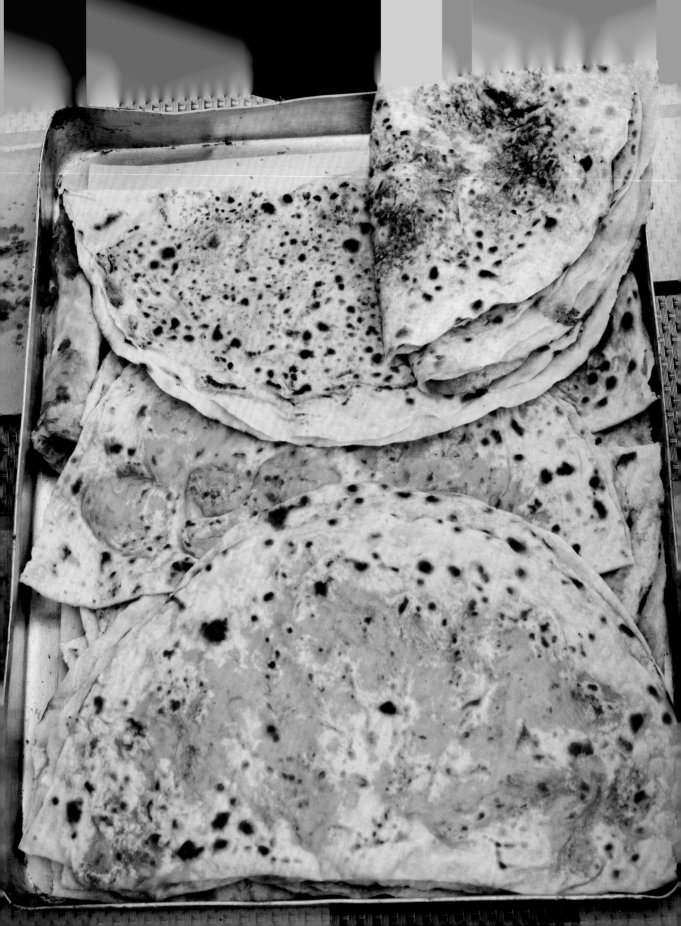

LAHMACUN

Lahmacun (pronounced 'lah-ma-june') literally means 'meat with dough' and is often referred to as Turkish or Armenian pizza. I first encountered them in Gaziantep in the Syrian border. Made with minced lamb and baked in the oven there, they sprinkled them with lemon juice and a handful of parsley and rolled them up before eating. This one is made with the addition of chickpeas, red pepper and green chilli.

MAKES TWELVE

1 quantity *Flatbread dough*
   (page 307)
Olive oil, for greasing
Plain flour, for dusting

For the topping
1 red pepper, deseeded
   and roughly chopped
1 green chilli,
   roughly chopped
1 medium onion,
   roughly chopped
5g/1 clove garlic,
   crushed or grated
600g minced lamb
Small handful flat-leaf
   parsley, finely chopped
1½ tsp chilli flakes,
   plus extra to serve
1 tbsp tomato paste
200g jar or tin
   chickpeas, drained
Salt
Lemon half

Place the dough in a clean, lightly oiled bowl, cover with cling film and leave to rise for about 30 minutes to an hour until doubled in size.

To make the topping, put the red pepper, green chilli, onion and garlic into a food processor and blitz until finely chopped but not pulverized. Tip into a sieve or on to kitchen paper and squeeze out any excess liquid.

Put the minced lamb in a bowl and add the red pepper mix, parsley, chilli flakes, tomato paste, chickpeas and a little salt. Mix well with your hands, being careful not to crush the chickpeas to a pulp, then set aside.

Heat the oven to 240°C/gas 9. Punch the dough down and knead again until smooth, then divide into 12 balls. On a lightly floured surface, roll each ball into a disc or an oval about 3mm thick and place on baking sheets. Top each with a twelfth of the topping mixture and spread with the back of a spoon, right to the edges.

Bake for 7–8 minutes until the top is sizzling and the base is lightly browned. Squeeze over a little lemon juice before serving. Serve with an extra pinch of chilli flakes if you like it really spicy.

GRIDDLED MACKEREL IN A BAGUETTE WITH TOMATO, LETTUCE, ONION, CHILLI & SUMAC

Balık ekmek

If you have been to Istanbul, I am certain you will have had one of these sandwiches from a kiosk near the Galata Bridge over the Golden Horn. What I love about the combination is not just the delicious sandwich but the little plastic cup of pickles and pickle juice you get to go with them (see page 102). *Recipe photograph overleaf*

MAKES FOUR

4 mackerel fillets,
    seasoned with salt
Olive oil, for frying
2 baguettes
1 onion, halved
    and finely sliced
1 tsp sumac
¼ tsp salt
3 tomatoes, sliced
Lemon half
Large handful chopped
    Little Gem lettuce
1 tsp Turkish red pepper
    flakes or ½ tsp chilli flakes

In a large frying pan over a medium heat, warm a little olive oil and pan-fry the mackerel fillets for 3 minutes on each side.

While they are cooking, cut the baguettes across into 2 and slice open. Put the onion slices in a bowl and toss together with the sumac and salt.

Lay some tomato slices on each bottom piece of bread, top with a mackerel fillet, squeeze over some lemon juice, finish with lettuce, onion and red pepper or chilli flakes, and cover with the top crust. Serve immediately.

TURKISH PICKLES

Turşu

Served alongside grilled meat and stuffed flatbreads as well as balık ekmek, the fish sandwich on page 99. Use the same pickling ingredients to preserve whole chillies.

MAKES A 1-LITRE JAR

For the vegetables
650g total weight of any
   combination of the
   following vegetables:
Carrots, cut in half
   lengthways and widthways
Radishes, halved
Spring onions, trimmed
Mini courgettes, halved
   lengthways
Fennel bulb, sliced
Cauliflower florets, sliced

For the pickle
Small handful fennel herb
250ml water
1½ tsp salt
1 tbsp sugar
250ml white wine vinegar
1 tsp coriander seeds
1 red chilli, sliced, seeds in

You also need
1 litre Kilner-type jar,
   sterilized by being warmed
   in the oven at 140°C/gas 1
   for 30 minutes

Heat the oven to 140°C/gas 1. Leave a clean, 1-litre Kilner-type jar in the warm oven for 30 minutes to sterilize it.

Pack the vegetables into the sterilized jar along with the fennel herb.

In a saucepan, bring the water to the boil then dissolve the salt and sugar in it. Add the vinegar, coriander seeds and red chilli. Pour over the vegetables in the jar and seal. Store for a few weeks before eating.

SAUTÉED LAMB'S LIVER IN FLATBREADS WITH CHILLI, CUMIN, RED ONIONS & SUMAC

It's a shame that we seem to have lost our affection for offal dishes. I know, for example, that every time I mention kokoretsi (see page 90) which, in its native form, is lamb's lungs, heart, kidneys and liver wrapped in the entrails and slowly cooked over hot coals, people recoil in horror, when in fact it is delicious. The Turks have no such aversion.

SERVES SIX

½ quantity *Flatbread dough*
(page 307)
Olive oil, for greasing

For the liver
30g plain flour, plus
    extra for dusting
1 tsp chilli flakes
1 tsp ground cumin
1 tsp dried oregano
1 tsp salt
3 turns black peppermill
500g lamb's liver,
    trimmed and cut
    into 1cm-thick slices
1 large or 2 medium red
    onions, halved and
    thinly sliced
1 tsp ground sumac
30ml olive oil
15g/3 cloves garlic,
    crushed or grated
Small handful flat-leaf
    parsley, roughly chopped
2 tomatoes, sliced
Handful of lettuce,
    torn or shredded

Make the dough as described on page 307, place in a clean, lightly oiled bowl, cover with cling film and leave to rise for about 30 minutes to an hour until doubled in size. Put baking sheets or pizza stones into the oven and heat to 230°C/gas 8.

Season the flour with chilli flakes, cumin, oregano, salt and pepper. Add the liver and toss well, making sure they are evenly coated.

Mix the onion slices with the sumac, then set aside while you make the flatbreads and cook the liver.

Punch the dough down and knead again until smooth, then divide into 6. Roll each out with a rolling pin on a lightly floured surface into a rough circle about 3mm thick. Transfer each to a hot baking sheet/stone and bake for 5–7 minutes, in batches if necessary.

Heat the olive oil in a frying pan and fry the garlic for about 30 seconds. Add the coated liver and fry briefly over a high heat on both sides. You want the outside cooked and crispy and the inside pink and soft. Add half the chopped parsley and remove from the pan.

Spoon sliced onions on to the flatbread and top with spicy liver, chopped parsley, sliced tomato and lettuce, and serve immediately.

LAMB & PISTACHIO KÖFTE

For these you really do need a flat metal skewer, the sort of thing that you are bound to buy in a shop somewhere in Turkey on holiday and then find again a year or two later languishing in the back of the garage. You need the surface area to enable you to turn them. If you use a thin, round skewer, the meat will fall off. This is what I would call the epicentre of Turkish cuisine. Köfte are popular all the way from Greece to Iran and as far as India, but the combination of fennel, coriander and cumin with minced lamb, pistachio nuts and chilli flakes sums up Turkey.

MAKES EIGHT TO TEN

1 tsp cumin seeds
½ tsp fennel seeds
½ tsp coriander seeds
1.2kg minced lamb
Handful flat-leaf
    parsley, chopped
1 tsp dried mint
2 eggs, beaten
10g/2 cloves garlic,
    crushed or grated
75g pistachios,
    roughly crushed
1 tsp chilli flakes
1 tsp salt
3 turns black peppermill
Juice 1 lemon
Plain flour to bind,
    if necessary
Olive oil, for brushing

To serve
Pide (page 32),
    Cacık (page 35)
    and a simple salad

Crush the spice seeds with a pestle and mortar, then mix all the ingredients together. If the mixture is too wet, add a little plain flour. Form with wet hands into sausage shapes on metal skewers. Brush with a little oil.

Cook on a charcoal barbecue or under a hot grill for about 8 minutes, turning regularly, until cooked through.

Serve with pide bread, cacık and salad.

SPICED LAMB FILO PASTRIES WITH RED ONION, CINNAMON & CUMIN

Börek

These thin pastry parcels are as ubiquitous in Turkey as pork pies and pasties in the UK. They can be made into triangles or cigar shapes and the fillings can be adjusted to taste: you could add rice, currants, fresh chopped chillies, pistachios or even walnuts. Here I've made them into triangles.

MAKES SIX OR TWELVE

12 sheets filo pastry
75ml olive oil or melted
    butter, for brushing

For the filling
400g minced lamb
1 tbsp olive oil
1 small red onion, chopped
5g/1 clove garlic, grated
1 tsp ground cinnamon
½ tsp ground cumin
1 tsp chilli flakes
1 tsp dried mint
2 tbsp tomato paste
½ tsp salt
3 turns black peppermill
20g pine nuts
Small handful flat-leaf
    parsley, chopped

Start by preparing the filling. In a frying pan over a high heat, brown the minced lamb all over before reducing the heat to medium and adding the olive oil, onion, garlic, spices, dried mint and tomato paste. Cook for 15–20 minutes, adding a little water if necessary, but you want a fairly dry mixture. Season with salt and pepper and stir through the pine nuts and parsley.

Heat the oven to 200°C/gas 6. Take 1 sheet of filo, brush it with olive oil (or melted butter), then top with another layer of filo. Keep the rest under a tea towel or cling film to prevent drying out while you work. Cut the 2-layer filo into 2 long strips and stack these up so you have a 4-layer strip.

Place a spoonful of mixture at the thin end nearest to you. Fold a corner of the dough across to form a triangle. Brush with a little oil or melted butter and fold upwards. Continue folding, across then up, until you reach the end of the strip of pastry. Repeat with the rest of the filo and filling until you have 6 triangular parcels. Alternatively, make 12 small parcels by cutting the 2-layer filo into 4 long strips.

Brush with a little more oil or butter, place on baking sheets and bake for 10–12 minutes.

★★★
MEAT

This chapter does feature some rich, meat-laden dishes for high days and holidays, but mostly the cooking from this region is all about a small amount of meat and a lot of vegetables, pasta, pilaf or pizza.

❧

This chapter does feature some rich, meat-laden dishes for high days and holidays, but mostly it's all about a small amount of meat with lots of vegetables or carbohydrates in the shape of pasta, pilaf or pizza, or small pieces cooked on skewers over charcoal, in the shape of souvlakis or kebabs.

But on those high days the meat of choice is lamb. I have to admit I've probably got one too many slow-cooked lamb or goat dishes in this chapter, but they're so good I just couldn't leave them out. The Turkish lamb tandir (page 145), cooked traditionally in their equivalent of a tandoori oven is, I would suggest, the dish that brings tears to a Turk's eyes when he is a long way from home. So too for the Albanians would be tave kosi baked lamb (page 143) with yogurt and rice. For the Greeks it would have to be kleftiko (page 140), a dish which is so simple and yet so close to a Greek's heart, that to hear them speak of it kindles a fire in one's own, to experience it as they do.

I think of the Mediterranean diet as being one of olive oil, garlic, sweet onions and tomatoes, scented cucumbers, deeply coloured aubergines and peppers and sweet fish out of a salty sea. I almost forget that they love meat too. A feature common to the Dalmation Coast, Greece and Turkey is the meat stew, and characteristically these are almost more about the other ingredients than the meat. In the introduction to Mooj's stew on page 123, I say I liked it because it has many vegetables. Actually, initially I thought there were too many.

Cooking in this region is often about eking out precious meat with lovely accompaniments. Nothing is more efficient and welcoming than pasta, whether it be a ragu bolognese in Ravenna, the sporki macaroni in Croatia or delicious dumplings called manti – spiced beef in pasta dough, with a chilli and yogurt sauce – in Turkey.

GRILLED STEAK WITH VILLAGE MUSHROOMS

The Greeks have a particular way of cooking mushrooms, which at first I wasn't sure about, but now I am. First they sauté the mushrooms, then add vinegar. It is just a case of not putting too much in. It occurred to me, after I had cooked the mushrooms to my complete satisfaction with a bit of balsamic vinegar, that they would make a perfect accompaniment to steak done on the barbecue and sprinkled with oregano and lemon juice.

SERVES FOUR

4 rib-eye or sirloin steaks
    (about 250g each)
50ml olive oil, plus
    extra for brushing
Salt and freshly ground
    black pepper
2 tsp dried oregano
Lemon half
200g button mushrooms,
    thinly sliced
25g/5 cloves garlic, chopped
25ml balsamic vinegar

Brush the steaks with olive oil, season with salt, pepper and half the oregano and grill on a barbecue or under a grill on a heat high until done to your liking. Squeeze lemon juice over the cooked steak.

In a frying pan, sauté the mushrooms in the 50ml olive oil with the garlic, balsamic vinegar, ½ teaspoon salt, 20 turns of the black peppermill and the rest of the oregano. Serve alongside the steak.

BEEF WITH OXYMELI

I have to say, I have worked on this dish somewhat. The original recipe contained far too much vinegar and orange juice. 'Oxymeli' refers to an ancient dish, a trilogy of ingredients – orange, vinegar and honey – traditionally used in northern Greece in meat stews. Whether this was for flavour enhancement or for disguising less-than-special meat is arguable, but used with discretion it does add a satisfying flavour to a stew.

SERVES SIX TO EIGHT

50ml olive oil
1.2kg chuck steak,
    cubed and seasoned
    with salt and pepper
1 large onion, halved
    and sliced
15g/3 cloves garlic, sliced
300ml full-bodied red wine
25ml red wine vinegar
100ml freshly squeezed
    orange juice (about
    2 oranges)
Zest 1 orange
1 tsp cumin seeds
1 large sprig rosemary
75ml honey
2 tsp salt
Freshly ground
    black pepper

Heat the olive oil in a large pan over a high heat and brown the beef cubes in batches. Reduce the heat to medium, return all the browned meat to the pan along with the onion and garlic, and cook for 5 minutes, then add the remaining ingredients. Bring to a simmer, cover with a lid and cook gently for 1½ hours until the beef is tender.

PATRICK LEIGH FERMOR'S MOUSSAKA

Having read the late Patrick Leigh Fermor's travel book called *Mani, Travels in the Southern Peloponnese*, I jumped at the chance of visiting his house in Kardamyli. The book is a glorious, rambling account of the rugged people and terrain of this very dry part of the mainland, with constant digressions into archaic learning, including the little-known fact that the Courtenay family of Powderham Castle in Devon were related to one of the Byzantine emperors. I spoke to his housekeeper, Elpida, who agreed to cook me the moussaka loved by the great man. She said she offered to cook it for him one day, but he said he didn't like moussaka. She made it anyway and served it without telling him what it was. 'That was really nice. What was it?' he said. Hence this recipe, and its name. And it is very nice. She fries everything separately first, including the potatoes, which don't always come as part of a moussaka. Put in the base of the dish, the potatoes act like a sponge, soaking up all the meat juices released during cooking.

SERVES SIX TO EIGHT

Salt
1 aubergine, sliced lengthways
3 courgettes, sliced lengthways
About 300ml olive oil
2 large potatoes, peeled and sliced lengthways
2 small onions, chopped
10g/2 cloves garlic, chopped
750g minced beef
3 beefsteak tomatoes, chopped
1 cinnamon stick
1 bay leaf
12 turns black peppermill

For the béchamel
100ml butter
100g plain flour
750ml full-fat milk
3 eggs
¼ tsp grated nutmeg
150g graviera cheese (or Gruyère if unavailable), freshly grated

Begin by salting the aubergine and courgette slices and leaving them for about 30 minutes, then rinse and dry on kitchen paper. Fry in plenty of the olive oil over a medium heat until lightly browned and starting to soften, then drain on kitchen paper and set aside. Fry the potatoes in the same way.

In a separate pan, heat 70ml of the olive oil and fry the onions and garlic for 5 minutes until softened. Add the minced beef and brown it before adding the tomatoes, cinnamon stick, bay leaf, 1½ teapoons salt and the pepper. Simmer for 30–40 minutes. When done, remove the cinnamon and bay leaf.

In a deep ovenproof dish, about 24cm x 35cm, arrange the potatoes in a layer. Top with a third of the beef, then the aubergine, another third of the beef, the courgettes, and finish with the remaining beef.

Heat the oven to 220°C/gas 7. Make the béchamel sauce: melt the butter in a saucepan over a gentle heat, stir in the flour and cook for 2 minutes so it loses its raw taste. Slowly incorporate the milk, and continue stirring until the sauce thickens. Remove from the heat and whisk in the eggs, nutmeg and 100g of the grated cheese. Spread the béchamel over the layered meat and vegetables and top with a further 50g grated cheese. Bake for 30 minutes, then take out and leave to cool. Serve warm. The dish is also very good the following day.

SPORKI MACARONI

Sporki means 'dirty', which doesn't sound right as a recipe title. What it does mean, though, is a rugged beef sauce that just coats pasta and, yes, dirties it. This recipe, which comes from Kopun restaurant in Dubrovnik, would be very well accompanied by the local red wine made from the plavac mali grape, which reappears in Puglia in Italy as primitivo, and is also closely related to zinfandel.

SERVES SIX TO EIGHT

30ml olive oil
400g lean beef, cut into
    pieces 1cm x 2cm
3 small red onions, chopped
3 small carrots, sliced
1 bay leaf
Salt
20 turns black peppermill
2 tbsp tomato paste
½ tsp ground cinnamon
10g/2 cloves garlic,
    finely chopped
300ml *Chicken stock* (page 307)
300ml full-bodied red wine
600g pasta tubes, penne,
    long macaroni or similar
Handful fresh
    parsley, chopped

Heat the olive oil in a large pan over a high heat and brown the chunks of beef in batches. When done, return all the meat to the pan, lower the heat, add the chopped onions and carrots and stir.

When the onions and carrots are brown, add the bay leaf and season with 2 teaspoons of salt and the pepper. Stir in the tomato paste, cinnamon and garlic and fry gently for a couple of minutes before adding the chicken stock and the red wine. Bring up to a simmer, cover with a lid and cook for 50–60 minutes, until the beef is tender.

About 15 minutes before you plan to serve, add the pasta to plenty of boiling salted water and cook until al dente. Drain the pasta and add to the meat with the chopped parsley. Stir well and allow to cook over a low heat for about 10 minutes to combine all the flavours.

POT-ROASTED BEEF WITH RED WINE, PRUNES & BACON

Pašticada

I guess you could call this the national dish of Croatia. The combination of this deep fruit-laden stew with some of the red wine called Dingač would probably bring tears to the eyes of these romantic people far away from home. The key to a great pašticada is the balance of sweet from the fruit, in this case prunes, and the red wine and balsamic vinegar. It is also important to choose a cut of meat with lots of connective tissue to add moistness during the long, slow cooking process; I suggest silverside. We spent two weeks on the island of Symi in Greece where I cooked about four dishes a day. We had no problem with fish, vegetables or fruit, or lamb for that matter, but beef from a country not used to cooking it in this way proved a problem. I made this and was quietly depressed about the dryness of the meat, which I suspect was topside. We filmed a short dialogue between me and David, the director, in which he said, 'I don't mean to be rude but it was a bit dry,' and I had to admit that it was.

SERVES SIX TO EIGHT

1.5–2kg silverside beef joint
20g/4 cloves garlic,
    sliced lengthways
50g smoked bacon lardons
60ml balsamic vinegar
1½ tsp salt
6 turns black peppermill
125ml olive oil
3 medium onions, quartered
3 sticks celery, sliced
3 carrots, sliced
750ml red wine
2 apples, peeled and
    cut into eighths
8 prunes
3 tomatoes, chopped
1 tsp sugar
1 sprig thyme
2 bay leaves
1 small sprig rosemary
Gnocchi, to serve

Pierce the meat with the point of a sharp knife and insert slivers of garlic and bacon lardons into the slits. Place the beef in a dish, pour the vinegar all over it, cover and leave for an hour or two.

Heat the oven to 160°C/gas 3. When ready to cook, season the beef with the salt and pepper. Heat a couple of tablespoons of the olive oil in a flameproof casserole pan over a high heat, add the beef and brown it all over. Then add the remaining olive oil, the onions, celery, carrots and red wine, and bring up to the boil. Cover with the lid, transfer to the oven and cook for about an hour.

Remove from the oven and add the apples, prunes, tomatoes, sugar and herbs, and a little water if looking at all dry. Return to the oven to cook for another hour with the lid on, until the meat and vegetables are tender.

Take the meat, vegetables and fruit from the sauce and keep warm. Reduce the sauce if required, and taste and check the seasoning. Carve the meat into 1cm-thick slices and serve with the sauce and gnocchi.

MOOJ'S MEDITERRANEAN BEEF & VEGETABLE STEW WITH NOODLES

Mooj (Müjde) runs a country restaurant near Selçuk with rather deluxe rooms and a delightful herb garden. It also houses a cookery school, and she is famous on Turkish TV for her cooking. There is nothing complicated about this stew, but I really liked it because it is more about the vegetables than the beef. There was a very attentive waiter called Apo (Abdullah) from Syria, whose family had been recently killed and whom she had taken under her wing. *Recipe photograph overleaf*

SERVES SIX

4 tbsp olive oil
2 leeks, cut into 4cm chunks
2 aubergines, in 4cm chunks
2 carrots, in 4cm chunks
2 onions, in wedges,
    root end intact
2 shallots, halved
3 courgettes, in 4cm chunks
1 large red pepper, deseeded,
    in 4cm chunks
200g green beans,
    in thirds lengthways
100ml red wine
2 tbsp tomato paste
2 tbsp *Red pepper paste*
    (page 307)
150ml passata
1 tsp chilli flakes
1 tsp dried oregano
1½ tsp salt
12 turns black peppermill
500g chuck steak, cut
    into 3–4cm pieces
2 large tomatoes, sliced
Sprig rosemary, leaves
    detached and chopped

For the noodles
200g 00 pasta flour,
    plus extra for dusting
Salt
2 eggs, beaten
55g tulum peyniri or pecorino
    romano cheese, grated

Heat the olive oil in a large, flameproof casserole pan and sauté the chunks of vegetables for about 5 minutes. Then add the red wine, tomato and red pepper pastes, passata, chilli flakes, oregano, salt and pepper. Put the chunks of beef on top and press them down into the vegetables slightly. Arrange the slices of tomato over the beef and sprinkle with rosemary. Bring up to the boil, then turn down to a very gentle simmer and put a lid on the pan. Cook for about 1½ hours or until the beef chunks are tender.

For the noodles, mix the flour, ½ teaspoon of salt and the eggs to 'breadcrumbs' in a food processor, then tip on to a lightly floured surface and bring together to form a dough. Knead for 3–4 minutes until smooth and elastic. Wrap in cling film and rest for half an hour before rolling.

Divide the pasta into 2 pieces and roll out into long, 2mm-thick sheets, using a rolling pin or with a pasta machine. Cut into tagliatelle-style ribbons. Use a little extra flour if required to prevent sticking.

Cook in boiling salted water for 2–3 minutes, until tender, then drain and serve, sprinkled with grated cheese, alongside the stew.

TURKISH DUMPLINGS
Mantı

Mantı, star-shaped dumplings, are the Turkish equivalent of tortellini, but whereas in Italy they would be served with a cream or tomato sauce, in Turkey the sauce was always going to be yogurt with a spicy chilli oil poured on top. The filling is spiced beef.

SERVES SIX TO EIGHT

For the dough
400g 00 pasta flour,
  plus extra for dusting
4 eggs, lightly beaten
Salt

For the filling
450g minced beef
Small handful parsley
Small handful oregano
5g/1 clove garlic,
  crushed or grated
½ medium onion,
  finely chopped
1 tbsp tomato paste
1 tsp chilli flakes
12 turns black peppermill
1 tsp salt

For the yogurt dressing
200g natural yogurt,
  loosened with
  a little water
¼ tsp salt

For the chilli dressing
2 tsp dried mint
2 tbsp *Red pepper paste*
  (page 307)
4 tbsp olive oil

In a food processor, combine the flour, eggs and 2 teaspoons of salt, then tip on to a lightly floured work surface and bring together into a ball of dough. Rest for 20 minutes.

Combine all the ingredients for the filling.

With a pasta machine or a rolling pin, roll out the pasta into a couple of thin sheets about 2mm thick. Using a pizza cutter or a knife, cut into 5cm squares.

Place a teaspoonful of the filling in the centre of each square, then, using your fingers, bring opposite corners up to meet on top in a star shape. Pinch with your fingers to neatly the seal the edges of the pasta cushions. Continue until all the dough and filling is used. Leave to dry on baking parchment on a tray, until ready to cook.

Bring a pan of salted water to the boil, then turn down to simmer, add the pasta and cook for about 4 minutes. Mix the ingredients for the yogurt and chilli dressings. Drain the pasta and serve immediately with the yogurt dressing poured over and the chilli dressing drizzled on top.

PASSATELLI

To me, passatelli is a bit like bagna cauda in that a small amount is wonderful but it is too rich for a larger helping. Bagna cauda, incidentally, is a warm olive oil, garlic and anchovy dip for fresh vegetables. Passatelli is made with a rich beef stock, lots of Parmesan and bone marrow. It's well worth making and serving in tiny portions, like one of those courses in a tasting menu in a three-star restaurant. The few mouthfuls will speak to you eloquently about the superbly rich cooking of Emilia-Romagna.

SERVES EIGHT TO TWELVE

For the brodo (broth)
2.5 litres water
900g shin of beef
750g marrow bones
2 carrots, roughly chopped
2 sticks celery,
    roughly chopped
2 onions, in wedges
50g piece Parmesan rind
2 bay leaves
2 sprigs thyme
1 tsp salt

For the dough
200g Parmesan cheese
    seasoned for 24
    months, grated
200g white breadcrumbs
3 eggs, lightly beaten
2 tbsp beef marrow
    (see *Brodo* above)
16 rasps nutmeg
Zest ½ lemon

To make the brodo, bring the water to the boil in a large pan or stockpot. Add all the brodo ingredients, bring back up to the boil, turn down to a simmer, skim off any scum and simmer gently for 2½ hours. Strain the liquid and set aside until ready for use. Scoop the marrow from the beef bones and use it in the dough.

To make the passatelli dough, place all the ingredients in a food processor and mix until it forms a ball of dough. Wrap in cling film and rest for 1–2 hours in the fridge. Using a potato ricer or grater, rice or grate the mixture into strips.

Reheat the brodo to hot but not boiling, add the passatelli strips, turn off the heat and allow the passatelli to sit in the hot broth for a few minutes before serving.

RAGÙ BOLOGNESE

I haven't in any way modified this recipe, which came from the kitchen of the
Radisson Blu hotel on the outskirts of Ravenna. I just wanted to present it exactly as
it was. The recipe is the chef's grandmother's. I think Bolognese is number one or two
in our own nation's favourite dishes. I have to confess I have always been a bit po-faced
about loading lots of sauce on top of the pasta, but here they do exactly that, before
transferring it to serving dishes with grated Parmesan on top. *Recipe photograph overleaf*

SERVES SIX TO EIGHT

1 stick celery, finely chopped
2 carrots, finely chopped
1 medium onion,
    finely chopped
60ml olive oil
300g minced beef
300g lean minced pork
100g smoked bacon
    (as lean as possible),
    finely chopped
1 tsp salt
15 turns black peppermill
100ml Sangiovese wine
60ml water
500ml passata
2 tbsp tomato paste
1 sprig rosemary

To serve
450–600g tagliatelle or
    spaghetti, freshly cooked
Parmesan, freshly grated,
    to taste
Freshly ground black pepper

In a heavy-based pan, fry the celery, carrots and onion
in the olive oil for about 10 minutes.

Add the beef, pork and bacon and brown, stirring
occasionally. Season with the salt and pepper, and add the
wine, water, passata, tomato paste and rosemary. Continue
cooking over a low heat for approximately 2 hours with
a lid on the pan.

Serve with tagliatelle or spaghetti, topped with freshly
grated Parmesan.

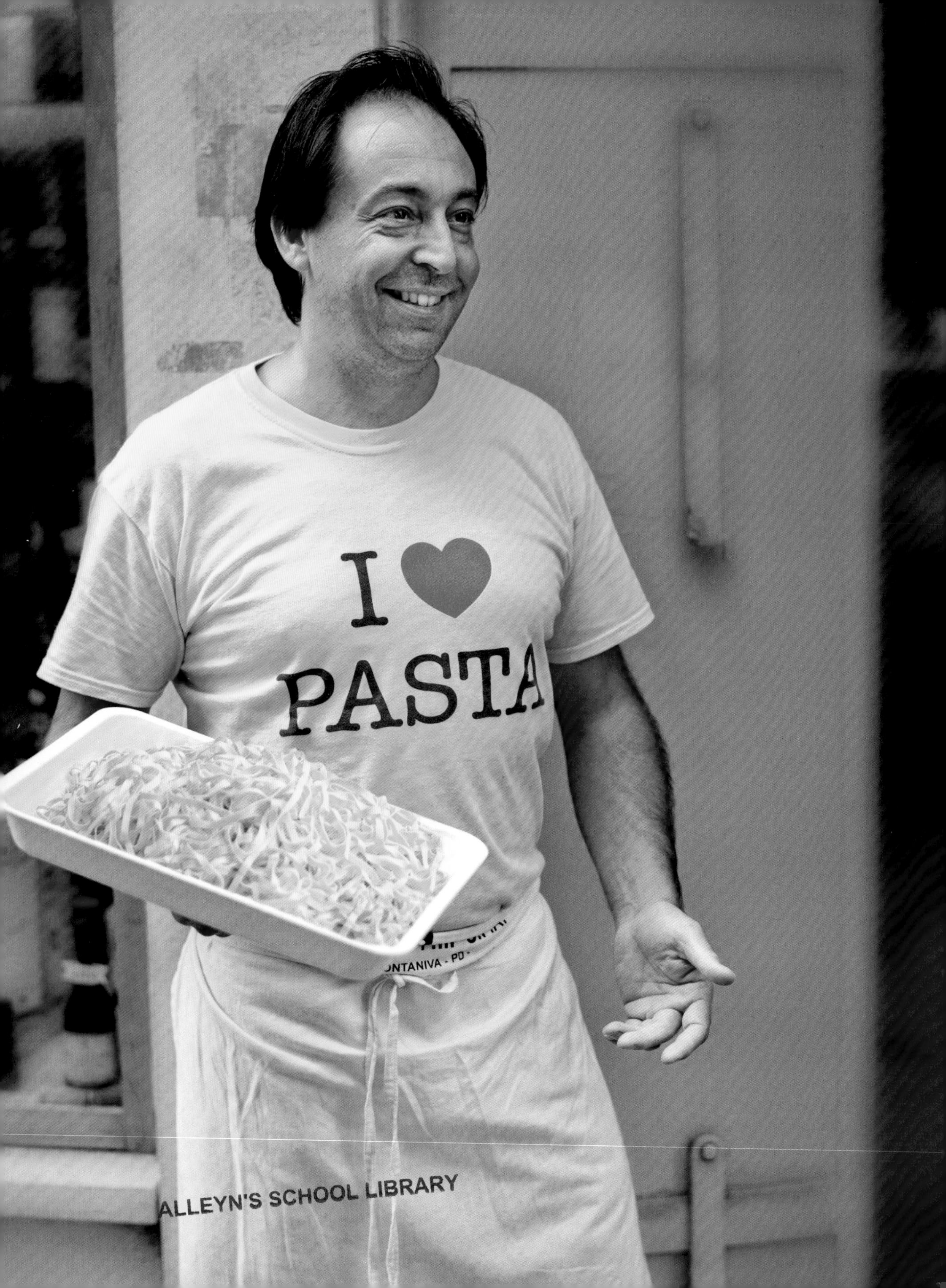
I ♥
PASTA

QUICKLY COOKED CALF'S LIVER WITH ONIONS & PARSLEY
Fegato alla veneziana

I prefer the calf's liver in this classic Venetian dish to be cooked quickly, but the onions need slow cooking to produce their lovely sweetness. Quite often the liver comes well cooked, as it did at the Food and Art Café in Giudecca where we filmed. They do a three-course lunch for 12 euros and serve dishes such as sarde in saor (see page 64). The chef, Irene Fortunato, cubed rather than sliced the liver and thoroughly cooked it. However, it was perfectly nice, and in a city famous for astronomical prices this is a fabulous off-piste place to visit, where students and workers from nearby shipyards flock every lunchtime.

SERVES FOUR

600g calf's liver, trimmed and any thin membrane removed, then cut lengthways into slices (ask your butcher to do this for you, if you like)
75ml olive oil
450g small onions, halved and thinly sliced
Sea salt and freshly ground black pepper
30g butter
Small bunch flat-leaf parsley, chopped

For the Parmesan polenta
900ml water
115g polenta (cornmeal)
40g butter
75g Parmesan cheese, finely grated
Salt

For the Parmesan polenta, bring the water up to the boil in a medium-sized pan. Pour in the polenta in a slow, steady stream, stirring all the time, then bring to a simmer and leave to cook gently, stirring frequently, for 20 minutes.

Meanwhile, cut the slices of liver across at a slight angle into short strips about 2.5cm wide.

Heat 3 tablespoons of the oil in a large, heavy-based frying pan over a medium-high heat. Add the onions and cook for 10 minutes, stirring frequently, until they are soft and a deep golden brown. Transfer to a bowl and keep warm.

Add another 1½ teaspoons of the oil to the pan and return it to a high heat. When the oil is sizzling hot, add a quarter of the liver and some seasoning and cook for 30 seconds, stirring constantly, until lightly browned. Tip on to a plate and repeat three times with the remaining liver.

Return all the liver to the pan with the onions and any juices from the plate and toss over a high heat for another 30 seconds. Spoon on to a warmed serving platter. Add the butter to the pan and scrape up any browned bits from the base; remove from the heat and stir in the chopped parsley. Spoon over the liver and onions.

Add the butter, Parmesan cheese and a little salt to taste into the polenta. To serve, put the polenta on to warmed plates and spoon some of the liver and buttery juices on top.

VEAL PEKA

Memories for me here of the macho end of the cooking spectrum. We travelled up into the hills behind Split to a village and a restaurant that specialized in spit-roasting lambs. Lovely guys but you wouldn't want to be on the wrong side of an argument with them, the way they pushed a metal spit through a freshly slaughtered lamb's carcass and out through the head with teeth spitting everywhere. The restaurant is legendary in Croatia. Loads of pictures featured the family with Croatian celebrities and stars from abroad. The lamb was exceptional but I couldn't really write a recipe for it. Where would you get the equipment? But they did a very nice pot-roasted dish on the embers of a wood fire, called a peka. The name refers to the pan itself, which has a domed lid that they cover with hot coals so the food cooks from above as well as from underneath (see page 110). They cook lamb and veal this way. I have chosen the veal version; osso buco is what you ask for at the butcher's.

SERVES SIX

Vegetable oil, for greasing
2 tomatoes, roughly chopped
1.5kg veal shank pieces
    (osso buco)
2 tsp salt
20 turns black peppermill
1 small celeriac, peeled and
    cut into rough chunks
1 small swede, cut into
    rough chunks
2 carrots, cut into
    rough chunks
10 small potatoes,
    cut in half lengthways
2 small onions,
    cut in half lengthways
Small handful
    rosemary leaves
100ml dry white wine
100ml water
100ml olive oil

Heat the oven to 200°C/gas 6. Select the option for top and bottom heat, if you have it, to emulate the cooking method traditionally used.

Grease the base and sides of a large, high-sided casserole pan with the vegetable oil, then add the chopped tomatoes. Put in the veal pieces and season with the salt and pepper, then add the root vegetables, onions, rosemary, white wine, water and olive oil. Put the lid on and cook in the oven for about 45 minutes. Turn the meat and baste in the fat and juices, then cook for a further 30 minutes with the lid off.

Test that the veal is tender and browned with juices concentrated to form a thick sticky sauce. If it's too dry, add a little more water; if too wet, reduce the liquid a little. Serve hot.

VEAL STIFADO WITH BULGUR WHEAT SALAD

I really liked Marina Siarava. She was the second of two cookery students we met in Ioannina (see page 208), one of the most famous seats of learning in Greece. Both had lost their jobs and were re-training. She was very lively, liked a glass of red wine and a cigarette, and wanted to open a theatrical restaurant with an open-plan kitchen where the chefs communicate using mime and the sounds of their pans and knives chopping are picked up on microphones as part of the ambience of the place, perhaps even with a DJ doing the mix. It sounds wacky stuff, but I have learnt that ideas like this suddenly become the next big thing, so I am not sceptical. And actually the stifado is delicious, as is the bulgur wheat salad.

SERVES FOUR

For the stifado
65ml olive oil
700g boneless veal leg,
   cut into 5cm chunks
1 medium onion, chopped
250ml red wine
3 large tomatoes,
   peeled and chopped
1 each long or bell red and
   green pepper, chopped
150ml water
5 allspice berries, crushed
1 cinnamon stick
1½ tsp sea salt
10 turns black peppermill
12 small red onion or shallots,
   peeled and left whole

For the bulgur wheat salad
250g bulgur wheat, rinsed
500ml boiling water
Large handful flat-leaf
   parsley, mint and
   dill, chopped
5g/1 clove garlic, thinly sliced
1 each red and green pepper,
   finely diced
1 tsp sea salt
1 tbsp olive oil

Heat 50ml olive oil in a large frying pan over a high heat and brown the veal in batches, then transfer the meat to a lidded, flameproof casserole pan along with another tablespoon of olive oil. Add the chopped onion to the casserole pan and fry for a few minutes over a medium heat.

Add the red wine, bring to a simmer and allow it to reduce a little before adding the chopped tomatoes, peppers, water, allspice, cinnamon stick and salt and pepper. Put the lid on, bring up to the boil, then turn down to a low heat and cook for 45 minutes.

Add the small onions or shallots and continue to cook for a further 45 minutes, being very careful when stirring not to break the onions apart.

Meanwhile, put the bulgur grains in the boiling water and set aside for 25 minutes to absorb the water and swell. Drain the bulgur wheat of any remaining water, transfer to a serving bowl and add the herbs, garlic and peppers. Season with the salt and drizzle with the olive oil, and serve alongside the veal stifado.

VEAL CANNELLONI

The fact that lots of recipes in Croatia are Italian can work against my including them in the book. However, if it is something I really want, like this cannelloni, I am only too pleased to include it. I have loved cannelloni ever since I was little. My parents used to take me to a long-gone restaurant in Soho called the Venezia – I don't know if there was anything particularly Venetian about it – and I loved the unfamiliar taste of Parmesan, the white sauce and tomato and the smoothness of the veal and spinach stuffing.

SERVES SIX

250g dried cannelloni tubes
300ml *Tomato sauce* (page 307)

For the filling
650g minced veal
1 onion, finely chopped
20g/4 cloves garlic,
    crushed or grated
45ml olive oil
150ml dry white wine
2 tbsp tomato paste
2 tsp salt
15 turns black peppermill
300g fresh spinach, wilted
    over a medium heat,
    drained and chopped
15 rasps nutmeg
50g Parmesan cheese, grated

For the béchamel sauce
75g butter
125g plain flour
1 litre full-fat milk
1 bay leaf
50g Parmesan or pecorino,
    freshly grated

For the filling, combine the veal, onion and garlic in a food processor and whizz until you have a coarse paste. In a large frying pan over a high heat, warm the olive oil, add the veal mixture and cook until browned all over. Add the white wine, tomato paste, salt and pepper and continue to cook, covered with a lid, for 20–30 minutes. Stir in the spinach, nutmeg and Parmesan.

Make the béchamel sauce: in a saucepan over a medium heat, melt the butter and add the flour to make a roux. Cook for 2 minutes, then remove from the heat and slowly add the milk, whisking to avoid lumps. Return to the pan, add the bay leaf and continue to stir until thickened. Season with half the Parmesan or pecorino and set aside.

Heat the oven to 180°C/gas 4.

Spoon a ladleful of the béchamel sauce in the base of a large greased rectangular baking dish. Take each cannelloni tube and spoon some of the veal into it. Continue until all the pasta and filling is used.

Arrange the cannelloni in a single layer in the dish and pour the tomato sauce over. Cover with the remaining béchamel, top with the rest of the grated cheese and cook for about 40 minutes. Leave the dish to rest for 5 minutes before serving.

LAMB KLEFTIKO

I have written a recipe for kleftiko before, but this one, based on one we had in a restaurant in Symi, had to go in the book. I think it was the combination of tomatoes, red pepper and waxy potatoes and a whole bulb of garlic that did it, plus the slow cooking. Any leftover lamb is delicious wrapped in a warm flatbread with lettuce, tomatoes and finely sliced onions, and perhaps cacık from page 35.

SERVES EIGHT

1.5kg waxy potatoes, peeled and cut into wedges
1 large red pepper, deseeded and cut into strips
3 large tomatoes, cut into thick slices
1½ tsp salt
12 turns black peppermill
1 leg of lamb (about 2.5kg)
Juice 1 lemon
60ml olive oil
1 bulb garlic, cut in half horizontally
1 tbsp dried oregano
200ml water
100g feta cheese, roughly crumbled

Heat the oven to 190°C/gas 5. Place the potatoes, red pepper and tomato in a large, flameproof oven dish or tin and season with the salt and pepper. Put the leg of lamb on top and pour over the lemon juice and olive oil, then add the garlic halves to the dish. Sprinkle all over with the oregano. Pour the water into the dish and cover with foil, sealing the edges well to retain the moisture as it cooks. (A large enamelled, lidded, cast-iron pot, such as Le Creuset, would also be suitable to cook this in.)

Cook in the oven for 2½–2¾ hours until the meat is falling off the bone, adding a little more water, if necessary, halfway through to keep the vegetables moist. Remove the foil (or lid) and add the feta, then return to the oven for 10 more minutes. After this time, check the consistency of the juices. If the dish seems a little dry, add a little more water. If too dilute, transfer the meat and vegetables to a serving dish and reduce down the liquid on the hob.

Serve the meat in chunks or thick slices with the vegetables and juices.

LAMB KOKKINISTO WITH PASTA

I am fascinated by what people in another country cook all the time, and this is one of those dishes. We asked our fixer in Monemvasia to find a family with a reasonable standard of living to cook us something. Out we went to the village of Aggelona. I was rather amused because it was one of those Greek houses with the next storey awaiting construction and the reinforcement bars sticking up, but inside it was very comfortable. A husband, wife and a couple of kids, a lovely kitchen garden outside, a nice kitchen inside, lamb stew, with bucatini added at the end as is so often the case. I know it sounds boring, but Greeks are just nice people.

SERVES SIX

60ml olive oil

750g boned shoulder of
    lamb, cut into 3cm cubes

1 medium onion, chopped

10g/2 cloves garlic, sliced

1 green pepper, deseeded
    and sliced

125ml white wine

1 bay leaf

¼ tsp ground cinnamon

¼ tsp ground allspice

3 turns black peppermill

½ tbsp tomato paste

300ml passata

¼ tsp sugar

1 litre water

1 tsp salt

500g spaghettini or bucatini

75g mizithra or pecorino
    cheese, grated

Heat 1 tablespoon of the olive oil in a large pan over a high heat and brown the lamb in batches. Pour off any excess lamb fat from the pan. Set the lamb aside.

Add the remaining olive oil to the pan and the onion, garlic and green pepper. Cook for about 5 minutes until they are starting to soften, then add the white wine, bay leaf, spices, tomato paste, passata and sugar, along with the browned lamb and 200ml of the water. Simmer, covered with a lid, for 30 minutes, then taste and add the salt.

Remove the lamb from the sauce, cover with foil and keep in a warm oven.

Add the remaining 800ml water to the pan and bring to the boil. Add the pasta and cook until al dente in the sauce. Combine with the lamb in a large serving bowl and serve with grated cheese.

ALBANIAN BAKED LAMB WITH RICE
Tavë kosi

Tavë kosi is a national dish in Albania, but I only had it once, at a restaurant at the top of a mountain pass at Llogara. I wasn't predisposed to like it. Lamb with rice and yogurt doesn't immediately appeal, but it turned out to be very good indeed, the same sort of dish as a moussaka (see page 118). I have made it a couple of times since then, and I have found the perfect accompaniment is a simple lettuce salad. This is a very satisfactory midweek dinner, especially if you have hungry kids at school – so I am told by Portia, the home economist I work with, who luckily has two teenage children, Will and Florence, who are very good at telling us exactly what they think.

SERVES EIGHT

70g butter
1 tbsp olive oil
1.2kg boned shoulder of
    lamb, cut in 5cm cubes
Salt and freshly ground
    black pepper
20g/4 cloves garlic, grated
1 tsp dried oregano
200ml water
60g long-grain rice, rinsed
50g plain flour
600ml Greek-style yogurt
4 eggs, beaten
Nutmeg

Heat 20g of the butter and the olive oil in a large pan over a high heat and brown the lamb in batches. Return all the lamb to the pan, add the garlic, oregano and water, bring to a simmer and cook, covered with a lid, for about 45–60 minutes until the lamb is tender.

Stir in the rice, and season with 2 teaspoons of salt and 12 turns of the black peppermill. Transfer to a 3-litre earthenware or other ovenproof dish.

Heat the oven to 180°C/gas 4. Melt the rest of butter (50g) in a small saucepan, add the flour and make a roux, cook for 2 minutes, then take off the heat. Add the yogurt and mix well, then return to the heat and cook gently for a couple of minutes. Take off the heat, add the beaten eggs and season with salt and pepper to taste.

Pour the sauce over the lamb and rice mixture, grate fresh nutmeg on top and bake for 40–45 minutes until starting to turn golden. Remove from the oven and allow to sit for 5 minutes before serving.

LAMB TANDIR

Lamb tandir was traditionally made in a tandoor oven (tandir), but I presume only when the heat for the charcoal was beginning to dissipate, because for success it needs a long, slow cooking. When it's good, there is nothing better, but many times it can be on the dry side. In Turkey they make it with a whole leg, but with our lamb it would only really work with the shank; the rest of the leg tends to be too dry after long cooking.

We filmed it being made at the Barbun restaurant in Alaçatı, and it was extremely succulent. I wonder if their lambs, which are smaller than ours, are more sinewy, and therefore turn gelatinous through slow cooking. For this reason, I prefer to use a shoulder. Serve with Turkish rice or spiced pilaf, cacık (see pages 269, 268 and 35) and salads.

SERVES SIX TO EIGHT

1.5–1.7kg shoulder of lamb
2 large carrots,
   roughly chopped
1 large leek, sliced
40g/8 cloves garlic,
   peeled and left whole
50ml olive oil
Juice ½ lemon
1 tsp salt
10 turns black peppermill
1 tsp dried oregano
2–3 rosemary sprigs, leaves
   detached and chopped
200ml water

Heat the oven to 190°C/gas 5. Score the lamb in a diamond pattern. Place the carrot, leek and garlic cloves in a large, flameproof oven dish or tin, and put the lamb on top. In a bowl, mix the olive oil, lemon juice, salt, pepper, oregano and rosemary. Pour the mixture over the lamb, rubbing it into the meat. Pour the water into the dish and cover with foil, sealing the edges well to retain the moisture as it cooks. (This could be cooked in a large enamelled cast-iron pot, such as Le Creuset, with the lid on.)

Cook in the oven for 2½–3 hours until the meat is falling off the bone, adding a little more water, if necessary, halfway through to keep the vegetables moist.

Remove the foil (or lid). Turn on the grill or top heat in the oven and brown the top of the joint. Strain the juices and keep warm to serve as gravy. Pull the meat apart using two forks, and serve with the gravy on the side.

TURKISH SPICED CABBAGE & MINCED LAMB STEW WITH TOMATOES

Kapuska

You have to make this. Portia Spooner, who works with me on the recipes, has cooked it half a dozen times. She laments the fact that so many British children don't like cabbage, which she says is because it is always just boiled. This recipe, which comes from a tradesmen's restaurant in Istanbul, makes cabbage delicious. I went to the restaurant with a knowledgeable and enthusiastic food blogger called Tuba Şatana. She wanted me to have the lamb tandir, which was outstanding, but I chose kapuska too. I often like to choose a cabbage dish because other countries, notably India and China, do some wonderful things with the humble brassica, and this is in the same class. Serve with crusty bread.

SERVES FOUR

45ml olive oil
250g minced lamb
2 medium onions, chopped
8g/1 large clove
    garlic, chopped
1 tbsp tomato paste
1 tbsp *Red pepper paste*
    (page 307)
½ tsp chilli flakes,
    plus extra to serve
4 tomatoes, peeled
    and chopped
1 tsp salt
6 turns black peppermill
375ml water
1 medium Savoy or white
    cabbage, coarsely chopped

Heat 1 tablespoon of the olive oil in a large pan over a high heat and fry the minced lamb until brown all over. Reduce the heat to medium, add the rest of the olive oil, the onions and garlic, and stir until softened.

Add the tomato paste, red pepper paste, chilli flakes, chopped tomatoes, salt and pepper, and cook for a few minutes until the tomatoes start to break down. Add 250ml of the water, bring to a simmer, put a lid on the pan and cook for 30 minutes.

Add the cabbage and the rest of the water, and simmer for another 30 minutes. Sprinkle with a large pinch of chilli flakes and serve.

RICH LAMB STEW
WITH AUBERGINE PURÉE
Hünkar beğendi

In my book on Spain there is a recipe from Navarra called chilindrón, which is a lamb stew with a lot of hot pimentón. It is possibly my favourite dish in the book, such a very Spanish take on slow-cooked lamb. I think hünkar beğendi will be the same sort of dish in this book. Again, it is spicy with a fair bit of tomato in it and cooked until the sauce is thick and unctuous, but what makes it special is the aubergine purée. I have had the dish many times in Turkey and sometimes the purée has been put through a food processor and becomes rather too smooth; for me it has to be mashed with a fork, and if there are flecks of the charred skin in it, I don't mind. It needs some grated cheese. I have suggested Parmesan but mizithra or possibly kasseri would be more authentic if you can get it.

SERVES FOUR

For the lamb stew
4 tbsp olive oil
850g boned shoulder of
    lamb, cut into 3cm cubes
1 tbsp *Red pepper paste*
    (page 307)
2 tbsp tomato paste
1 onion, chopped
12g/2 large cloves
    garlic, chopped
1 green finger chilli, sliced
1 green pepper, deseeded
    and sliced
3 tomatoes, peeled
    and chopped
1 tsp dried oregano
1 tsp salt
6 turns black peppermill
200ml hot water
Flat-leaf parsley, to serve

For the aubergine purée
4 medium aubergines
30g butter
30g plain flour
380ml full-fat milk
75g grated Parmesan cheese
Juice ½ lemon
Salt and black pepper

Heat the oven to 220°C/gas 7. Put the aubergines on a baking tray and bake whole for 25 minutes. When soft, remove from the oven and leave to cool.

In a large flameproof casserole pan over a high heat, warm half the olive oil and brown the lamb in batches. When browned, return all the lamb to the pan, add the red pepper and tomato pastes, the remaining olive oil, and the onion, garlic, chilli and green pepper. Reduce the heat to medium and cook until softened. Add the chopped tomatoes, oregano, salt and pepper, and finally the hot water. Bring up to a simmer then turn down the heat, cover with the lid and allow to cook slowly for 1–1½ hours.

When cool enough to handle, peel the aubergines and mash the flesh with a fork. In a pan over a medium heat, make a roux: melt the butter, add the flour and cook, stirring, for 2 minutes, then add the milk to give a thick white sauce. Mix in the aubergine, the grated cheese and lemon juice, and season with salt and pepper. Keep warm.

When the lamb is tender, check the sauce: it should be rich and thick. If it's too runny, remove the lamb and reduce the liquid a little, then return the meat to the pan and warm through. Chop some flat-leaf parsley. Serve the stew on top of the aubergine purée, scattered with parsley.

LAMB & POTATOES
WITH LEMON

When I watched this being cooked in a wood-fired oven, I thought it was going to be a bit dull. It's not. The potatoes in particular have a lovely lemony flavour.
Recipe photograph overleaf

SERVES FOUR TO SIX

1.5kg chunks lamb
    rump on the bone
4 large potatoes
1 tsp salt
16 turns black peppermill
1 tbsp dried oregano
Juice 1½ lemons
250ml olive oil
200ml water
A few sprigs rosemary
10g/2 cloves garlic, sliced

Heat the oven to 170°C/gas 3. Cut the chunks of lamb rump into 250g pieces. Peel the potatoes and cut into large chunks.

In a large roasting tin, mix the pieces of lamb with the potatoes, season with the salt, pepper, oregano and lemon juice, then pour over the olive oil, mixing well with your hands to coat the lamb.

Add the water to the tin together with sprigs of rosemary and the sliced garlic. Cover with foil and bake for 1¾ hours.

POT-ROASTED GOAT WITH POTATOES, ARTICHOKES & FENNEL

Yes, there are a lot of pot-roasted dishes in this book, but that is the nature of the cooking of Greece, Croatia and Turkey. This dish comes from a restaurant in Areopolis called Lithostroto Taverna. To me it was particularly good as I am very fond of wild fennel herb. Why is it that you can't buy it in the UK? I either have to grow my own or pick it in the hedgerows around Padstow. The cook, Maria, lines the bottom of a roasting tin about 4cm thick with fennel, then puts the goat leg steaks, cut through the bone, on top, followed by the potatoes and other vegetables, and finally the artichokes. It was a long, slow-cooked dish. We came back later that afternoon to a wonderful scene: a street in the old part of the town, a table right down it seating twenty or thirty people, the goat dish, the retsina, the red wine, the Greek salads, the green beans in tomato sauce – and about seventeen new Greek friends.

SERVES SIX TO EIGHT

1.5kg goat leg meat on the bone, cut into pieces (ask your butcher)
1.5kg new or waxy potatoes, cut into chunks
20g/4 cloves garlic, sliced
200g spring onions, chopped
200g wild garlic, chopped
10 artichoke hearts, freshly trimmed or from a jar
100ml fresh lemon juice
1 tbsp tomato paste
2 tbsp passata
2 tsp sea salt
12 turns black peppermill
1 tbsp mustard powder
2 tsp sugar
150ml water
Large handful fennel herb
150ml olive oil

Heat the oven to 150°C/gas 2. Place the goat meat in bowl, and add the potatoes, garlic, spring onions, wild garlic and artichoke hearts. Mix together the lemon juice, tomato paste, passata, salt, pepper, mustard powder, sugar and water and pour over the meat. Leave to marinate for a couple of hours.

Place the fennel leaves in the bottom of a rectangular ovenproof dish. Arrange the meat on top, the potatoes on top of that, and the artichokes around the sides. Pour the marinade all over and drizzle with the olive oil. Cook, uncovered, for 3 hours (or, if you prefer, cover with foil for 2 hours, then remove for the final hour). Allow to cool for 5 minutes, then serve.

KID GOAT STEW WITH PEAS

When I watched Biliana make this dish, there was an awful lot of goat and peas involved. She was actually cooking about twenty-five portions of it to serve in her restaurant that evening. It is a shame we don't eat more goat here, because once you get used to it, you grow to like it a great deal. It is like lamb, but not quite. We have lost enthusiasm for peas that have past the fresh bloom of youth, thanks to the complete dominance of frozen petits pois. There is a lovely pulses quality in fresh but not youthful peas, which I think I have captured by using dried marrowfat peas, the stuff of mushy peas in fish and chip shops. This is a very good dish. Don't be put off by its simplicity.

SERVES FOUR

100ml olive oil
225g onions, halved
  and sliced
200g smoked
  pancetta, chopped
1kg kid goat leg meat on
  the bone, cut into pieces
  (ask your butcher)
200ml white wine
1 tsp sea salt
6 turns black peppermill
8 cloves
200ml *Tomato sauce*
  (see page 307)
800ml hot water
1 tbsp sweet paprika
Small handful
  parsley, chopped
250g dried marrowfat
  peas, soaked in water
  overnight, drained
  and rinsed

Heat the olive oil in a large flameproof casserole pan over a high heat, add the onions, pancetta and pieces of goat on the bone and brown them. Then add the white wine and season with the salt, pepper and cloves. Add the tomato sauce and 300ml of the hot water, the sweet paprika and chopped parsley, and cook for 45 minutes.

After this time, add the rest of the hot water (500ml) along with the soaked peas and continue to cook for 30–40 minutes, until goat and peas are tender. Allow to cool for 5 minutes, then serve.

SPLIT STUFFED AUBERGINES
Karnıyarık

The Turks do love a stuffed vegetable. In one restaurant in Istanbul, I had a red pepper, an aubergine, a gourd and a plum – it sounds like the hungry caterpillar, I know. These are similar to Greek versions stuffed with herbs and rice, but this is very Turkish, with pomegranate molasses and seeds, pine nuts, chilli and lamb. *Recipe photograph overleaf*

SERVES FOUR TO SIX

4 medium aubergines
5 tbsp olive oil, plus
    extra for drizzling
Salt and freshly ground
    black pepper
1 onion, finely chopped
12g/2 large cloves garlic,
    finely chopped
½ tsp pul biber
¾ tsp chilli flakes
1 tsp sweet paprika
1 tsp cumin seeds
2 tsp ground cinnamon
500g minced lamb
2 tomatoes, roughly chopped
2 tbsp tomato paste
50g pine nuts
Handful flat-leaf parsley,
    roughly chopped
175ml water
1 tbsp pomegranate molasses
Seeds 1 pomegranate

Heat the oven to 200°C/gas 6. Cut the aubergines in half lengthways and arrange in a roasting tin, cut side up. Drizzle with olive oil, season with salt and pepper and roast for 25 minutes. Remove from the oven and reduce the temperature to 180°C/gas 4.

Start to make the filling while the aubergines are cooking. Fry the onion and garlic in 3 tablespoons of the olive oil over a medium heat for 3–5 minutes until softened. Mix the paprika, pul biber, cumin seeds and ground cinnamon together and add two-thirds of this mixture to the pan, together with the chilli flakes. Fry for 1–2 minutes, then increase the heat and add the lamb. Cook until browned, then add the chopped tomatoes and 1 tablespoon of the tomato paste, the pine nuts and half of the parsley. Season with salt and pepper.

When the aubergines are ready, remove from the oven and carefully slit the flesh lengthways, without cutting all the way through the skin. Top each half with an eighth of the lamb mixture. In a bowl, mix the water with the remaining spice mix, olive oil (2 tablespoons), tomato paste (1 tablespoon) and the pomegranate molasses. Add this liquid to the roasting tin around the aubergines, cover the whole with foil and bake for 50–60 minutes, until the aubergines are soft and the juices in the pan are syrupy. Serve the aubergines drizzled with the pan juices and scattered with the pomegranate seeds and the rest of the parsley.

SLOW-COOKED PORK KNUCKLE & ONIONS

Before I go any further, it is worth pointing out that a pork knuckle is an economical cut of meat, the sort of joint you can put in a casserole over a very low heat, leave for four hours or so and it's done. This recipe comes from the Neraida restaurant just outside Neapolis, which describes itself as the taverna at the edge of Europe. The chef Pandelis was, I felt, very talented, one of those calm cooks who completely understands his local cuisine. The restaurant itself was like a Greek taverna from the 1970s: black-and-white shots of serious-looking men in suits doing labouring jobs, and an AMI Rowe jukebox in the corner with old Greek songs and, as Joni Mitchell would say about Matala in Crete in her song 'Carey', 'scratchy rock and roll'. I remember thinking, I wouldn't mind staying here for a few days – but the schedule wouldn't allow it. Filming has its downsides.

SERVES THREE TO FOUR

1.5kg knuckle of pork
  (uncured)
5 cloves garlic, peeled
  and left whole
3 tbsp honey
250ml red wine
75ml olive oil
2 tsp sea salt
12 turns black peppermill
2 tsp mixed peppercorns:
  green, black, red
1 bay leaf
1 small cinnamon stick
1 tsp coriander seeds
75ml water

For the slow-cooked onions
400g red onions,
  halved and sliced
70ml olive oil
½ tsp salt
100ml water

For the tomato garnish
6 medium tomatoes, halved
3 tbsp olive oil
Pinch sea salt
6 turns black peppermill

Heat the oven to 120°C/gas ½. Make 5 small deep slits between the skin and flesh of the knuckle of pork using a sharp knife, and stud each slit with a whole clove of garlic. Rub the skin all over with the honey. Place in a casserole dish and add the red wine, olive oil, salt and pepper, peppercorns, bay leaf, cinnamon stick, coriander seeds and water. Cover with a lid and bring up to a simmer on the hob, then transfer to the oven and bake for 4–4½ hours.

While the pork is cooking, prepare the onions: sweat them in the olive oil for 5 minutes over a medium heat, then add the salt and water, cover with a lid and cook gently for 25 minutes.

Very gently cook the tomato halves in a separate pan with the olive oil over a medium heat for about 20 minutes until softened. Season with the salt and pepper. Serve the pork knuckle with the slow-cooked onions and tomatoes.

PORK SOUVLAKI WITH OREGANO
Kontosouvli

I enjoy the fact that quite a few people, when they have seen my TV programmes, go on a journey to visit the places I have been to. I particularly like the idea of Ioannina, in the region of Epirus in northern Greece, getting a few more visitors. It is beautiful and as yet not much frequented by British tourists, who prefer the whitewashed buildings and deep blue sea of the south. This recipe is my take on the kontosouvli, a souvlaki marinated in oregano and chilli, which we had at a restaurant that specialized in the souvlakis of Metsovo. Kontosouvli is best known from Cyprus, however, and is usually described as a souvlaki made with larger marinated pieces of pork; the ones we ate were only a little bit bigger than those of a standard souvlaki. I got nowhere asking for the recipe. I don't think they were being secretive; it's just that things don't always happen in Greece. The absolute must for a good souvlaki is great chips, and no one makes great chips like the Greeks (see page 308).

SERVES FOUR

400g pork shoulder,
 cut into 3cm cubes

For the marinade
30ml fresh lemon juice
2 tbsp olive oil
2 tsp dried oregano
½ tsp ground cumin
½ tsp cayenne pepper
1 tsp smoked paprika
 (pimentón picante)
3g/1 small clove
 garlic, grated
½ tsp salt

Mix all the marinade ingredients in a bowl and add the meat. Marinate for an hour or so, then thread the cubes of meat on to skewers. Grill on a barbecue or under a hot grill for 10–12 minutes, turning until cooked through.

PORK IN MILK

This is one of the dishes I really want people to try, even if, on first impression, you might think lots of milk and pork doesn't sound appetizing. What happens is that as you slow-cook the pork, which is two-thirds immersed, the milk curdles and gradually the liquid reduces until you are left with a ricotta-like cooked milk flavoured with fennel, garlic and sage. The pork is almost falling apart, so you serve it in 1cm-thick slices with the grainy sauce all around. It is totally wonderful, particularly if served with something bitter like the wilted radicchio on page 308 or a similar salad with anchovies and lemon on page 308. Polenta is the obvious carbohydrate to serve it with (see page 132).

SERVES EIGHT

2kg pork loin, skin and half thickness of fat removed, then rolled and tied
1½ tsp salt
6 turns black peppermill
30g butter
1 tbsp olive oil
30g/6 cloves garlic, crushed or finely chopped
6 sage leaves, torn
1 tbsp fennel seeds
Zest 1 lemon
1 litre full-fat milk
Juice ½ lemon

Season the pork all over with the salt and pepper. In a large flameproof casserole pan over a high heat, brown the pork on all sides in the butter and olive oil. Reduce the heat and add the garlic. Stir it briefly – don't allow it to burn – then add the sage leaves, fennel seeds and lemon zest.

In a separate pan, scald the milk: bring it to a simmer then turn off the heat.

Pour the scalded milk and lemon juice over the pork, bring up to the boil, then immediately turn down to a very gentle simmer, place the lid on slightly ajar and cook for 1½–2 hours. Turn the meat halfway through cooking. Keep checking every 20–30 minutes to ensure the milk is not burning on the bottom of the pan.

At the end of the cooking time the milk should be curdled and look like ricotta and the pork should be meltingly soft. Remove the meat from the pan, let it rest, covered, for 20 minutes, and check the sauce. If the sauce is not reduced enough, transfer to a clean pan and reduce down. Taste and season if necessary with salt. Serve the pork thickly sliced with the curdled milk sauce.

WALNUT-CRUSTED PORK CHOPS WITH FIGS

For this dish you make a paste of chopped walnuts, cinnamon, nutmeg and olive oil, coat the chops with it, fry them in butter, deglaze the pan with white wine, and add the dried figs and butter to make a delicious pan sauce. This recipe comes from Karen Evenden. She's an enthusiastic ambassador of Croatian cooking.

SERVES SIX

6 large thick-cut pork chops
Salt and freshly ground
    black pepper
½ tsp ground cinnamon
¼ tsp freshly grated nutmeg
100g walnuts, finely chopped
2 tbsp olive oil
40g butter, softened
125ml white wine
16 dried figs, finely chopped
125ml *Chicken stock* (page 307)

To finish
30g butter
1 tbsp flat-leaf parsley,
    roughly chopped
Juice ½ lemon

Season the pork chops with salt and pepper and score the flesh with a sharp knife. In a shallow roasting tin, mix the cinnamon, nutmeg and walnuts, add the olive oil to make a paste, and roll the chops in the nuts, pushing the crumb into the flesh.

Melt the butter in a large non-stick frying pan and brown the chops two at a time, being careful not to burn the walnuts. This will take a few minutes each side. Then return all the chops to the pan, cover with a lid and allow to cook through for about 10 minutes over a medium heat.

Remove the pork chops to a warmed plate and cover with foil to keep warm. Deglaze the pan with white wine, reduce by half, then add the chopped figs and chicken stock and season to taste. Whisk in the butter, parsley and lemon juice. Serve the pork chops with the sauce spooned over.

CROATIAN GREEN STEW
Zelena menestra

This dish comes from Korčula, famed as the possible birthplace of Marco Polo. It is great when nobody knows where a famous historical figure was born. It gives a lot of places the chance to stake a claim, which is wonderful for tourism. Korčula has more than enough natural beauty not to need anything else, but it all helps. This dish was made for me by Toni Lozica, who works at the most exquisite boutique hotel on the island, called Lešić Dimitri Palace. It was too expensive for a TV crew to stay in, but we very much liked the cheaper place we stayed in because they put on a quite amateurish but enjoyable half-hour of Korčulan music and dancing in the middle of the hotel buffet dinner.

SERVES EIGHT

900g ham hock
250g smoked bacon,
    in one piece
300g cooking chorizo
    sausages (about 4),
    skin pricked
700g new potatoes,
    peeled and left whole
1 small white cabbage,
    cut into 8 thick slices
    with the 'root' intact
300g cavolo nero, leaves
    cut into 4 pieces
Salt and freshly ground
    black pepper

Put the ham hock in a large pan, cover with water and bring to the boil, then turn down to a simmer and cook for an hour, skimming off any scum that rises to the surface.

Add the piece of bacon and chorizo sausages, and continue to cook slowly for 40 minutes.

Remove the meats from the pan, cover with foil and keep warm. Add the potatoes to the meat-cooking liquor and cook for 10 minutes. Add the white cabbage pieces and cook for a further 8–10 minutes. Lastly add the cavolo nero and cook for 2–3 minutes.

Drain the vegetables, reserving some of the cooking liquor. Check the seasoning of the liquor and, if necessary, season with salt and pepper. Cut the ham hock and bacon into 16 pieces each and slice the sausages. Arrange meat, potatoes, a slice of cabbage and a little cavolo nero on each plate, and drizzle over a few spoonfuls of the cooking liquor. Serve at once.

PASTA E FAGIOLI

This famous Venetian dish has a peasant-foody aroma about it that makes it probably the sort of thing you'd be massively enthusiastic about consuming after a brisk walk on a crisp December afternoon.

2 tbsp olive oil
1 large red onion,
    finely chopped
4 sticks celery, including
    leaves, finely chopped
1 medium courgette, chopped
5g/1 clove garlic, chopped
½ tsp chilli flakes
1 large sprig rosemary, leaves
    detached and chopped
70g pancetta, finely chopped
400g tin chopped
    plum tomatoes
125g dried borlotti or
    cannellini beans, soaked
    in water overnight and
    cooked, drained (reserve
    the cooking liquor)
125g mini macaroni
Sea salt

To serve
Good quality olive oil
Basil leaves, roughly chopped
Parsley or celery
    leaves, chopped
Freshly ground black pepper
Freshly grated
    Parmesan cheese

In a large heavy pan, heat the olive oil and fry the onion, celery and courgette over a medium heat. When softened but not browned, add the garlic, chilli flakes, rosemary and pancetta and cook for 2 minutes.

Add the tomatoes together with their juice and cook for about 20 minutes.

In a food processor or blender, purée half the cooked beans with a cup of their cooking liquor and add this to the tomato mixture with the whole beans. Add more of the bean-cooking liquor or 100ml water if the soup looks too thick.

In a separate pan, cook the macaroni in boiling salted water until al dente, drain and stir into the soup. Taste and add sea salt if required.

Serve with a generous helping of olive oil, chopped basil and parsley or celery leaves, black pepper and Parmesan cheese.

PORK STEW WITH SMOKED PAPRIKA & BORLOTTI BEANS

Groshe

Some of the philosophical questions of cooking: do you eat soup or drink it? When does a soup become a stew? When I first saw this simmering over a smoky wood fire in northern Albania, I couldn't make up my mind. Now, when I refer to a dish as earthy, I will always look back to that terracotta pot and the lovely smells of smoke, beans and cured pork.

SERVES FOUR

2 tbsp olive oil
1 onion, chopped
200g smoked streaky bacon, cut into 2cm chunks
1 tbsp smoked paprika (pimentón picante)
2 tbsp tomato paste
¼ tsp chilli flakes
½ tsp dried oregano
300g dried borlotti beans, soaked in water overnight, drained and rinsed
1.3 litres *Chicken stock* (page 307)
1½ tsp salt
6 turns black peppermill
Small handful flat-leaf parsley, chopped

Heat the olive oil in a large pan over a medium heat, add the onion and sweat for 3–5 minutes until softened, then add the bacon, paprika, tomato paste, chilli flakes and oregano and stir for a minute.

Add the borlotti beans and the chicken stock, bring up to the boil, then turn down to a simmer. Leave a lid on the pan slightly ajar and cook for 1½–2 hours until the beans are tender. Add a little water if the soup gets too thick. Season with the salt and pepper. Serve sprinkled with parsley.

RABBIT & ONION CASSEROLE
Lepur çomlek

I have been on the lookout for good rabbit dishes ever since I took a holiday on the island of Malta where there are a lot of them, being dry limestone country where not much other wildlife can thrive. This recipe, from Adriatic Croatia/Albania, uses garlic, tomatoes, olive oil, baby onions and red wine, and is best served with rice or orzo pasta.

Recipe photograph overleaf

SERVES TEN TO TWELVE

2 rabbits, cleaned and jointed
    (ask your butcher to do
    this, if you like)
3 bay leaves
4 tbsp balsamic vinegar
100ml olive oil
20g/4 cloves garlic, grated
6 whole allspice berries
1 cinnamon stick
200ml red wine
350ml *Chicken stock*
    (page 307), hot
2 tbsp tomato paste
5 ripe tomatoes,
    peeled and chopped
½ tsp dried oregano
2 tsp salt
10 turns black peppermill
600g baby onions or shallots,
    peeled and left whole
1 tsp sugar

Wash the rabbit pieces well, then pat dry and place in a bowl with the bay leaves and pour over the vinegar. Cover and set aside to marinate for at least an hour.

Heat the oven to 160°C/gas 3. Heat a couple of tablespoons of the olive oil in a flameproof casserole pan over a high heat and fry the rabbit pieces in batches until they are well browned all over. Return all the rabbit pieces to the pan along with the bay leaves from the marinade, then add the garlic, allspice berries, cinnamon stick and red wine. Bring to the boil, then add the chicken stock, tomato paste, chopped tomatoes, oregano, salt and pepper, and reduce to a simmer. Cover the pan, transfer to the oven and cook for 1–1½ hours until the rabbit is tender.

Meanwhile, heat the remaining oil in a frying pan and use to fry the baby onions gently, stirring frequently, until just golden all over (about 10–15 minutes), adding the sugar partway through to help them to caramelize. Tip the onions into the pot containing the rabbit just before it's done and stir through.

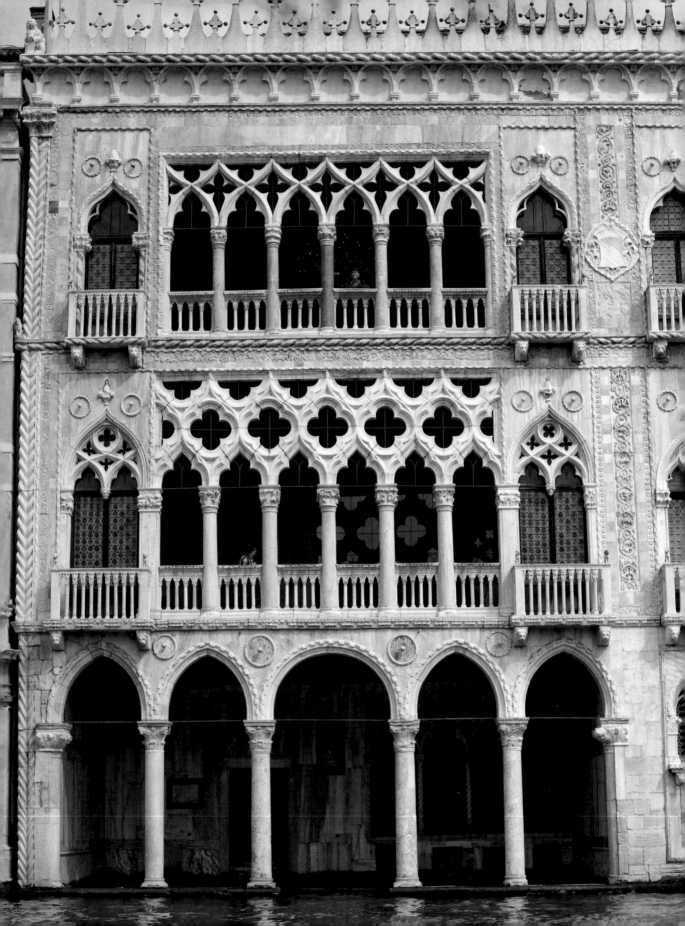

★ ★ ★ ★

POULTRY

You've got chicken pieces, nice and easy to get hold of, with lovely lemony sumac, chilli, pomegranate molasses, garlic and salt…

❦

I always like to hazard a guess which dish in a book of mine will be the most popular. Here I think it will be the oven-roasted chicken with sumac on page 185. It's incredibly easy to prepare and cook, and one glance at the dish says 'Turkey' to my mind. It might be what some would call a 'crowd pleaser': you've got chicken pieces, nice and easy to get hold of, with lovely lemony sumac, chilli, pomegranate molasses, garlic and salt. The stuffed duck from Venice, on page 197 is not in the same sort of crowd-pleasing category, but it is another of my favourites. Removing the bones from a whole bird before roasting it makes the serving very simple. Just the sort of thing you might consider for Christmas, and you can always ask your butcher to do the boning for you.

It's interesting, though, that this is one of the shortest chapters in the book. This is simply because there are not as many recipes for chicken or duck in the countries I visited as you might think, perhaps because chicken is not the mass-produced source of protein there that it has become elsewhere. The chickens in these countries are still pecking around in the yard. This is reflected in the taste of the meat. In Albania, for example, I found the chicken yufka on page 194 to be incredibly well flavoured, and I had to modify my recipe to allow for the fact that our own chickens lack something. The chicken with orzo recipe on page 184 was made with a rooster and the flavour was really quite strong, much like poulet de Bresse. These are like chickens used to be when I was young, when this meat was more eagerly anticipated than roast beef or lamb. I am afraid it's a bit of a sad statement about our poultry; there is just more flavour in theirs. We need more farm shops, I say.

THE BEST CHICKEN PIE IN GREECE
Kotopita

The Greeks love their pies almost as much as we or the Aussies do, but theirs are made by building up thin sheets of filo pastry. This chicken pie was sensational, made by a mother-and-daughter team, Iro and Virginia Papapostolu, in the village of Aspraggeli in the region of Zagori, a mountainous part of Epirus. The pie is made from a whole chicken. The chicken and onions are first poached, and the liquid then reduced to a gelatinous sauce. It is the sweetness of the onions that really counts here.

SERVES SIX TO EIGHT

1kg onions, chopped
30g butter
2 tbsp olive oil, plus
    extra for greasing
    and brushing
1 whole chicken
    (about 1.5kg)
3 eggs, beaten
1½ tsp salt
Freshly ground
    black pepper
6 sheets filo pastry

Put the onions, butter and olive oil into a large pan or stockpot with a lid, add the whole chicken and pour in enough water so the bird is almost submerged. Cover with the lid, bring the water up to the boil, then turn down to barely a simmer and poach the chicken for about 1½ hours.

When the chicken is cooked, remove from the pan and strain the cooking liquid into another pan, keeping the onions to return to the dish later. Boil the liquid hard to reduce to a tasty gelatinous stock. Allow the chicken to cool before stripping all the meat off the carcass, discarding the bones and skin. Put the chicken and the reserved onions into a large bowl and mix well. Add the eggs and chicken stock and season with the salt and some pepper.

Heat the oven to 230°C/gas 8. Grease a round pie dish with olive oil. Line the dish with 3 sheets of filo, alternating direction each time and brushing each layer with a little olive oil. Add the chicken mixture and fold the overhanging edges in. Top with a further 3 layers of filo, again placed at different angles to one another. Fold in the overhanging edges to seal the pie and brush all over with more olive oil.

Bake for 15 minutes. Remove from the oven, reduce the heat to 200°C/gas 6, cut the pie into 6 or 8 wedges, then bake for a further 45 minutes. Allow to rest for 10–20 minutes, then serve, still warm.

CHICKEN & TOMATO STEW WITH ORZO

When I had this at the O Nakos taverna in Koukounara, near Pylos, it seemed like the most simple recipe, everything in one pot: the pasta, in this case a rustic broken type called hilopites, the chicken and a tomato sauce. It proved to be much harder to get right, reinforcing my view that the simplest dishes are often the most difficult to cook – take note, all you guides to fancy food! I tried cooking it at a dinner at my house in Sydney and had to quietly throw it away as the pasta I was using, orzo, virtually dissolved into the sauce. My fault – I was talking to my guests too much. Possibly I should have realized this might happen. It is a dish that needs to be cooked and served immediately. I have now made this a number of times and finally cracked it, and it does, at last, fulfil its promise.

SERVES FOUR TO SIX

60ml olive oil
1 whole chicken (about 1.5kg),
    jointed into 8 pieces
1 medium onion, chopped
10g/2 cloves garlic, chopped
1 red pepper, deseeded
    and chopped
100ml red wine
1 litre *Chicken stock* (page 307)
500ml passata
7cm cinnamon stick
1 tsp dried oregano
1 tsp salt
12 turns black peppermill
300g orzo pasta
85g aged mizithra or pecorino
    romano cheese, grated

Heat the olive oil in a flameproof casserole pan over a medium-high and brown the chicken pieces. Reduce the heat, add the onion, garlic and red pepper and cook for about 5 minutes. Add the red wine, chicken stock, passata, cinnamon stick, oregano, salt and pepper. Bring to the boil, then reduce the heat, cover the pan with a lid and simmer for 20–25 minutes.

Add the pasta to the sauce, put the lid back on the pan and let it simmer for another 10–15 minutes. Serve at once, sprinkled liberally with grated mizithra or pecorino cheese.

OVEN-ROASTED CHICKEN WITH SUMAC, POMEGRANATE MOLASSES, CHILLI & SESAME SEEDS

This is an ideal chicken dish for an outdoor summer party. However, I favour cooking it in the oven because the marinade is apt to burn on a barbecue. I did it a couple of months ago at my holiday house by the water in Mollymook, NSW. I kept the heat low to avoid too much blackening but I needed to be at the barbie then, rather than chatting. Sumac is Turkey's favourite spice. It's a red berry with an astringent, lemony flavour, the fruit of a small bush. It's the sort of dish that's idea as part of a warm and cold buffet where people have a bit of everything including a rice pilaf. *Recipe photograph overleaf*

SERVES FOUR TO SIX

1 whole chicken (about 2kg),
  jointed into 8 pieces
3 tbsp olive oil
1 tbsp sesame seeds

For the marinade
2 tbsp ground sumac
12g/2 large cloves garlic,
  crushed or grated
½–1 tsp chilli flakes
1 tbsp tomato paste
1 tbsp pomegranate molasses
1 tsp salt

Mix all the marinade ingredients together, rub well into the chicken and leave for 1 hour.

Heat the oven to 200°C/gas 6. Put the chicken in a roasting tin, drizzle with the olive oil and scatter the sesame seeds over. Roast in the oven for 30 minutes.

CHICKEN WITH APRICOTS & ALMONDS
Mahmudiye

The coupling of fruit and meat in a slow-cooked stew is a great Byzantine tradition, that and the use of spices such as cinnamon and cumin.

SERVES SIX

30g butter
12 small shallots,
    peeled and left whole
2 tbsp olive oil
1kg chicken thighs
    (about 6 large) or
    750g skinless, boneless
    chicken thighs
1 cinnamon stick
Pinch ground cloves
Pinch saffron strands
1 tsp honey
Juice ½ small lemon
10 dried apricots,
    each sliced into 3
3 tbsp currants
1 tsp salt
12 turns black peppermill
250ml *Chicken stock* (page 307)
50g flaked almonds, toasted
Turkish rice (page 269),
    to serve

Melt the butter in a large sauté pan and gently fry the whole shallots until golden, about 10 minutes.

Add the olive oil and the chicken, and brown the chicken a little. Add the cinnamon stick, ground cloves, saffron, honey, lemon juice, apricots, currants, salt and pepper, and pour in the chicken stock. Bring up to the boil, then it turn down immediately until it is just simmering. Put a lid on the pan and continue to cook for 25 minutes, stirring once or twice.

Serve scattered with the toasted almonds, and Turkish rice alongside.

CIRCASSIAN CHICKEN

Çerkez tavuğu

A very attractive element in Turkish cuisine is their regular use of nuts in savoury dishes, particularly walnuts. I was lucky enough to be in a great market in Alaçatı this autumn. The types of fresh walnuts on sale indicated to me just how popular they are. I chose some that were nearly as big as eggs. The bitter membranes covering them were so fresh you could peel them off in one go. There cannot be many better flavours in this world than a white walnut without that darker skin. There is no real connection but I often describe the taste of fresh-caught herrings as being like fresh nuts. When Arezoo Farahzad, associate producer, sent me a brief description of Circassian chicken from Istanbul, I made it there and then, in my kitchen in Sydney, and gave it to some friends who came over for a drink. It was so Middle Eastern: the poached chicken in stock, and a sauce made with walnuts and garlic, then the oil and chilli on top.

SERVES THREE TO FOUR

2 large skinless
    chicken breasts
500ml *Chicken stock*
    (page 307)
200g walnut halves
1 slice stale white bread,
    made into breadcrumbs
10g/2 cloves garlic,
    crushed or grated
Salt
Small handful
    coriander, chopped

For the red pepper dressing
1 tbsp *Red pepper paste*
    (page 307) or ½ tsp
    sweet paprika and
    ½ tsp cayenne pepper
2 tbsp olive oil
¼ tsp salt

Begin by poaching the chicken breasts in the chicken stock. Bring up to the boil, then turn down to a simmer and poach for about 20 minutes or until cooked through.

In a food processor, blitz 150g of the walnuts (keep 50g of the nicest-looking halves) to a powder, then add the breadcrumbs and garlic, and enough of the poaching stock to create a creamy sauce. Season with salt.

Put the ingredients for the red pepper dressing in a bowl and whisk to combine.

Pull the chicken breasts apart into long pieces and combine with the walnut sauce and the chopped coriander. Drizzle with the red pepper sauce and stud with the remaining walnut halves.

A LIGHT CHICKEN STEW
WITH SPRING ONIONS

I got on very well with Janina and her husband Cengiz in Istanbul, and I was very pleasantly surprised, last half-term in Padstow, when they announced they were coming for dinner at the restaurant. So, over a bottle of extremely nice white Burgundy, we reminisced about Istanbul, which included memories of filming this lovely simple chicken stew with Janina in her kitchen, and a slightly boozy afternoon at the fish restaurant at İsmet Baba overlooking the Bosphorus.

SERVES FOUR TO SIX

30 spring onions, trimmed
40g butter
2 tbsp olive oil
2 carrots, cut into 2cm chunks
4 sticks celery, cut into
    2cm lengths
10g/2 cloves garlic, sliced
2 heaped tbsp tomato paste,
    loosened with a little water
2 tsp pomegranate molasses
1 tsp dried oregano
1 tsp salt
6 turns black peppermill
1 whole chicken (about 1.5kg),
    jointed into 6 pieces
300ml *Chicken stock* (page 307)
Small handful flat-leaf
    parsley, roughly chopped
Turkish rice or *Bulgur pilaf*
    (page 269), to serve

In a flameproof casserole pan over a high heat, brown the spring onions in the butter and olive oil. Lift them out of the pan and set aside while you brown the carrots and celery. Add the garlic, tomato paste, pomegranate molasses, oregano, salt and pepper, mix well, then add the chicken joints and return the spring onions to the pan. Pour over the chicken stock, bring to the boil, then reduce to a simmer, put the lid on the pan and cook for 30 minutes.

Serve scattered with chopped parsley alongside Turkish rice or bulgur pilaf.

CHICKEN YUFKA

We arrived in Albania in the middle of the night, crossing from Montenegro. This was not without alarm and paperwork. We were stranded at the border for two hours with no certainty we would be let in. I remember the two-hour journey from the border to the city of Lezhë, noticing how dim the lights were, a bit like rural India. I felt nobody could afford anything brighter. I woke up the next morning and travelled in the minibus into countryside I can only describe as Arcadia – beautiful pastures filled with wild flowers and herbs, a sense of somewhere lost in time, and a small, Slow Food-accredited restaurant, cooking everything in wood ovens, preserving roses, hand-making pasta and bread. Our host and chef, Altin Prenga, really did understand the purity and biodiversity of his countryside. I felt a sense of what we have lost in this country through modern farming methods. This is their signature dish, chicken with homemade pasta, baked in the oven. I have had to modify it a bit, but the most important element is the pasta part, cooked in homemade chicken stock and fresh sage.

SERVES FOUR

1 whole chicken
   (about 1.5kg),
   jointed into 8 pieces
2 tbsp olive oil, plus
   extra for greasing
Juice of ½ lemon
1 tsp oregano
½ tsp cayenne pepper
1 tsp salt
500g tagliatelle,
   broken in half
400ml *Chicken stock*
   (page 307)
4 fresh sage leaves
12 turns black peppermill

Heat the oven to 200°C/gas 6. Put the chicken pieces in a roasting tin and drizzle over the olive oil and lemon juice, then scatter with the oregano, cayenne and salt. Toss the pieces of chicken to make sure they are well covered. Roast for 20 minutes. Remove and set aside.

Meanwhile, cook the tagliatelle in boiling, salted water for 8 minutes, then drain and set aside.

Grease a large, deep roasting tin liberally with olive oil. Spread the cooked pasta over the base of the tin. Add the pieces of par-cooked chicken and all the juices in the tin. Pour the chicken stock on top, sprinkle with freshly torn leaves of sage and bake for about 10 minutes. You should be left with sauce that clings to the pasta. If it's too wet, reduce the liquid; if too dry, add a little more water or chicken stock. Season with the pepper and serve.

WARM VENETIAN SALAD

I have a friend in Sydney, Jennifer Rollins, who has lived in Italy, speaks the language fluently and has a complete love of a country whose climate is so similar to her own. At dinner one evening, she produced this recipe and the radicchio salad on page 308, and I was captivated by her understanding of what I, too, see in Italian cooking: a trust in great raw materials to deliver dishes that appear simple but are anything but. To me these two dishes, though not specifically Venetian, speak the same language of understatement. I purposely did not ask her for the recipes, just cooked dishes that reminded me of a great evening where love of good food briefly allowed us some respite from the fact that her husband Mark had recently died.

SERVES FOUR

1 large chicken breast,
   skin left on
1 tbsp olive oil
5g/1 clove garlic, chopped
4 spring onions, sliced
2 slices sourdough bread,
   torn into chunks
4 slices prosciutto,
   torn into strips
150g mixed rocket
   and frisée leaves
2 tbsp pine nuts, toasted
1 mozzarella ball,
   torn into chunks
1 ripe pear, sliced

For the dressing
1 tbsp red wine vinegar
2 tbsp *Chicken stock* (page 307)
2 tbsp olive oil
5g/1 clove garlic,
   crushed or grated
Salt and freshly
   ground pepper

Heat the oven to 190°C/gas 5. Roast the chicken breast for 20 minutes, then allow to cool a little. Remove the skin and tear the flesh into strips.

Heat the oil in a frying pan over a medium heat, sweat the garlic and spring onions until soft, then add to a large bowl with the chunks of sourdough and toss to coat.

Add all the other salad ingredients, including the chicken, to the bowl and toss. Whisk the dressing ingredients together, seasoning with salt and pepper, and drizzle over the salad just before serving.

STUFFED DUCK
Anatra ripiena

This is a dish of my own. I have found similar stuffings in dishes originating from the Veneto, but the idea of taking all the bones out of a duck, then rolling it round the same rich forcemeat, came from an Italian sous-chef who used to work for me, Jose Graziosi, who did about five geese like this for the staff Christmas tea on 24 December a few years ago. I have put a brief instruction in about how to bone a duck, but there are several companies on the internet that will do it for you, or ask your butcher. Alternatively, just use this as a stuffing for a duck, goose or turkey at Christmas.

SERVES SIX

1 whole duck, about 1.5kg
200ml water
1 tbsp plain flour
100ml red wine
250ml *Chicken stock*
   (page 307)
1 tbsp tomato paste
1 sprig rosemary

For the stuffing
½ medium onion,
   roughly chopped
45g butter
200g minced pork
Giblets from the duck
   (not the neck) or
   50g duck livers
200g pancetta or
   streaky bacon, sliced
Handful flat-leaf
   parsley, chopped
50g Parmesan, grated
½ tsp freshly grated nutmeg
1 tsp salt
20 turns black peppermill
1 egg

For the stuffing, gently sauté the onion in the butter until soft, then add to the bowl of a food processor with the rest of the ingredients and mince everything together.

To bone the duck, place the bird breast-side down and cut from the centre of the back to the tail and then to the neck. Work a thin-bladed, flexible knife under the skin of both sides, freeing first the leg, then the breast, without cutting the skin. Finally, cut the centre of the breast bone away from the skin, again avoiding cutting through. Remove all the leg and wing bones with a small knife. Lay the stuffing along the length of the back, and roll up and tie at 3cm intervals into a sausage.

Heat the oven to 150°C/gas 2. Set the duck on the wire rack of a roasting tin and add the water. Cook for 1.5–2 hours or until the meat temperature inside is 70°C but no more. Don't let all the liquid evaporate; add more water if necessary. Remove from the oven and allow to rest, covered, while you finish the sauce.

Pour the liquid out of the roasting tin into a jug. Drain off the fat but add 1 tablespoon back into a pan with the flour and stir over a moderate heat for 1–2 minutes. Add the strained juices, the red wine, stock, tomato paste and rosemary. Reduce to sauce consistency and pass through a sieve to remove the rosemary. Cut the duck into 1.5cm slices and serve with the sauce.

★ ★ ★ ★ ★
SEAFOOD

I could not have cared less about the fish skin being a bit broken – they were simply Mediterranean fish at their very, very best.

❧

One of the inevitable outcomes of filming anywhere in the world is people complaining about where you *didn't* go. In our Far Eastern Odyssey we didn't go to Korea, Laos or the Philippines. We went to Spain but didn't go to Portugal. In India we didn't go to Gujarat (my word, that has been a difficult one), and when we made Mediterranean Escapes we didn't go to Korčula. Not going to Korčula has been the bane of my life. So when David Pritchard, the director, and I came up with the idea of a long, rambling journey from Venice to Istanbul, part of the idea was to visit the island of Korčula and, inevitably, because life is like that, I had one of the most memorable seafood experiences there that I've had for a long time.

We found a little restaurant called the Bilin Zal, also the name of the beach, in a stone building by a jetty that was probably an old fish store. It had just opened for the summer season. Everyone to do with the restaurant was young and full of enthusiasm and excitement about the approaching summer trade. It reminded me of summer at The Seafood Restaurant years ago. The cook was a girl called Jelena in her early twenties. She grilled about a dozen small bream over charcoal and maybe it was because David, the director, was putting her under too much pressure or maybe because she didn't have enough experience, being so young, but the grill was not hot enough and the fish stuck to the bars and David was not amused – he can be a tad unsympathetic at times. The more crotchety he got – because obviously you need grill marks for the TV – the more disconcerted she became. But she kept smiling and she served the bream up with a lovely dish of lightly crushed new potatoes and green beans and olive oil, with a salad similar to a Greek salad, and I could not have cared less about the fish skin being a bit broken – they were simply Mediterranean fish at their very, very best.

GRILLED MACKEREL STUFFED WITH HOT RED PEPPER PASTE, PARSLEY & GARLIC

I wrote this recipe to honour the culinary reason for the existence of Istanbul.
A series of fishing villages in the Bosphorus were originally made prosperous by
enormous shoals of bonito, known in Turkey as palamut. Byzantium was the ancient
Greek city and precursor of Istanbul that was founded by Greek colonists drawn to
the area, I am sure, not just by its strategic position between the Mediterranean and the
Black Sea but also by the abundance of fish. Bonito is still a very popular fish in the city.
Go into any fish market in the autumn and bonito are displayed in glistening rows
with their bright red gills turned outwards so you can see how fresh they are. If you
can get hold of good chunky bonito, use it. Mackerel, however, is the closest thing
for the rest of us. Serve with a warm pilaf or grain salad.

SERVES FOUR

4 fresh mackerel
2 tbsp *Red pepper paste*
    (page 307)
2 tbsp pine nuts
2 tbsp tomato paste
30g/6 cloves garlic,
    finely chopped
1 onion, finely chopped
Handful flat-leaf parsley,
    finely chopped
1 tsp pomegranate molasses
Olive oil, for brushing

To prepare the mackerel, take a thin bladed, flexible
knife and cut just behind the head down to the backbone.
Don't cut through it. Turn the blade towards the tail, rest
your other hand on top of the fish and cut the fillet away
from the bones until you are about 3cm away from the
tail. Turn the fish over and repeat on the other side.
Pull back the top fillet and snip out the backbone close
to the tail, with scissors. The fillets will still be attached
by the tail. Discard the head and backbone.

Make a paste by mixing all the remaining ingredients.
Spreading a quarter over the inside of each mackerel.
Tie the fish at in three places along their length, brush
liberally with olive oil and grill on a barbecue or under
a hot grill for 4–5 minutes on each side.

FRIED RED MULLET
WITH ORANGES & CAPERS

The red mullet off Monemvasia are reckon to be the best in the Aegean. A net full of them, red yes, but pink too with flashes of yellow as the sun rose on a still dark blue sea is a lovely recollection, and fried for breakfast later they were quite memorable. A month later though, back in Padstow, I saw three autumn mullet landed at Newlyn in our fish shop. They were about twice the size with slightly deeper colours. I cooked them like I so often do with whole fish: seasoned, dusted with semolina and fried over a moderate heat in olive oil. I used to think the Mediterranean mullet were better than ours, but now I know the ones that come to Cornwall in autumn are pretty hard to beat.

SERVES FOUR

8 small or 4 medium
   red mullet, scaled
   and gutted
½ tsp salt
Freshly ground black pepper
Semolina, for dusting
50ml olive oil
2 small oranges: 1 zested
   and juiced, 1 thinly
   sliced into rounds
1 tbsp capers
1 tbsp pine nuts, toasted
Pinch chilli flakes
Small handful flat-leaf
   parsley, roughly chopped

Season the red mullet with the salt and some pepper, and dust with semolina. Heat the olive oil in a frying pan over a medium heat and fry the fish on both sides until golden. When done, remove to a plate and keep warm.

Deglaze the pan with the orange zest and juice, then add the orange slices, capers, pine nuts, chilli flakes and parsley to the pan and warm through. Pour over the fish and serve immediately.

TROUT WITH SPINACH & TOASTED ALMONDS

The fallout from the global financial crisis is particularly obvious in Greece, more so in the north than the south. In Ioannina two cookery students, Kostas Gerodimos and Marina Siarava, had lost good jobs; Kostas was a network technician and Marina was a designer for an architectural practice. Both were now learning to cook, and I liked the dishes they made. Kostas did local trout and kept it simple: new potatoes with dill, and the trout fried in olive oil and served with spinach, shallot, red pepper and flaked almonds. Marina's dish, a veal stifado with bulgur wheat salad, is on page 136.

SERVES TWO

2 trout fillets
Salt and freshly ground
  black pepper
Plain flour, for dusting
10 new potatoes
90ml olive oil
2 shallots, chopped
½ red pepper, deseeded
  and diced
200g fresh spinach, washed
50g flaked almonds
Juice 1 lemon
Handful dill, chopped

Season the trout fillets, dip in the flour ready to fry, then set aside.

Boil the new potatoes in their skins in salted water. When tender, drain and set aside to cool slightly, then halve and sauté in 30ml of the olive oil with some salt and pepper.

While the potatoes are cooking, fry the shallot and red pepper in a large frying pan in 30ml olive oil until soft, then add the spinach and turn down the heat to wilt; season. Remove from the pan and keep warm.

Wipe out the pan and dry-fry the almonds for 2 minutes to toast them, gently stirring until golden brown. Set aside.

Add the remaining 30ml olive oil to the frying pan and fry the trout fillets over a medium heat until golden on both sides. Season with the lemon juice while in the pan. Add the chopped dill to the potatoes.

To serve, place some of the spinach mixture on each plate, top with a trout fillet and the flaked almonds, with the sautéed potatoes on the side.

BREAM WITH CELERY
& AVGOLEMONO SAUCE

The Greeks use avgolemono not just in soup (see page 21), but also as a sauce for fish. It means 'egg and lemon'; used with the poaching liquor from celery and a few other green vegetables, it makes a surprisingly memorable accompaniment to a good gilthead bream. The recipe comes from Preveza, a seaside town on the western coast of Greece that is becoming a bit of a holiday destination. *Recipe photograph overleaf*

SERVES TWO

2 celery sticks, cut into 3–4cm
   lengths, and handful leaves
250ml water
2 sea bream, about 400g
   each, scaled and gutted
Handful fennel herb
Salt and freshly ground
   black pepper
4 tbsp plain flour
150ml olive oil
3 shallots, chopped
1 leek, chopped
1 egg
75ml *Fish stock* (page 308)
Juice 1 lemon

Poach the celery sticks in the water until just tender. Remove; reserve the water for use later.

Stuff the cavity of the fish with the fennel herb. Season, then dust both sides with flour. Heat half the olive oil in a frying pan and quickly fry on both sides until lightly golden (the fish are not being cooked through yet). Remove the fish to a plate.

Using the same pan, add the rest of the olive oil and fry the shallots, leeks and drained celery over medium heat for 2 minutes. Add the celery 'stock' and cook for a further 2 minutes. Put the fish back on top of the vegetables in the pan, cover and simmer for 20 minutes.

Beat the egg in a bowl. Take 4 tablespoons of the hot sauce from the pan and put in the bowl, whisking constantly. Add the fish stock, lemon juice and some seasoning, then return the mixture to the sauce in the pan with the fish. Serve immediately.

FISH BRODETTO
WITH BORLOTTI BEANS

To say this is a truthful account of the dish I watched being made in the Villa Spiza restaurant in Split would be inaccurate. Two sisters and their best friend, and one girl who seemed to be doing an awful lot of the work, drank large quantities of delicious Carić red wine and took about two hours to make this legendary fish stew. With apologies to Ivana and Nada, this is an attempt to recreate the flavour in a quarter of the time. I left with a nostalgia for the early days of The Seafood Restaurant, when friends would drop in and the wine was flowing and there was no thought of the hard grind and seriousness that was to come – not that we had young musicians playing like Stéphane Grappelli and Django Reinhardt in the street outside, like they did that afternoon.

SERVES EIGHT

Olive oil, for cooking
2 onions, halved and sliced
3 carrots, chopped
2 sticks celery, chopped
30g/6 cloves garlic, chopped
2 tsp salt
1 tsp chilli flakes
2 tsp smoked paprika
   (pimentón picante)
1kg dried borlotti beans,
   soaked in water
   overnight, drained
300ml dry white wine
2 x 400g tins chopped
   plum tomatoes
300ml prawn stock: see
   Petros's Clams (page 73),
   made with 8 large raw
   prawn heads, bodies
   reserved for the
   finished dish
Large handful flat-leaf
   parsley, chopped
1 bream, 1 bass and
   1 gurnard, scaled and
   gutted, then filleted

Heat 2 tablespoons of olive oil in a large pan over a medium heat. Add the onions, carrots, celery and garlic and cook for 3–4 minutes.

Add the salt, chilli flakes, smoked paprika, soaked beans, white wine, tinned tomatoes and prawn stock. Bring to the boil, then turn down to a simmer, cover with a lid and cook for 50–60 minutes or until the beans are tender, checking periodically and adding more water if necessary. When cooked, stir through three-quarters of the parsley.

Pan-fry the fish fillets and prawns over a medium heat in a little olive oil for 3 minutes each side. Place on top of the stew just before serving. Sprinkle with the remaining parsley.

BARBECUED SARDINES
IN VINE LEAVES

I swear you get some flavour from the vine leaf, and so I venture to suggest that this recipe is only for those with a vine growing in their garden, or with access to a Greek deli or about to go on holiday to a villa in the Med. The main reason for wrapping the fish, however, is to protect them and stop them sticking to the barbecue. This recipe comes from Çanakkale on the Hellespont, the nearest city to ancient Troy and just across the water from Gallipoli. *Recipe photograph overleaf*

SERVES SIX

12–18 fresh sardines
    (depending on size),
    scaled and gutted
Juice 2 lemons
1 tsp salt
1 tsp crushed white
    peppercorns
12–18 fresh vine leaves
    (1 per sardine)
150ml olive oil
Lemon wedges, to serve

Sprinkle the fish with lemon juice and season with the salt and white pepper. Soak the vine leaves in warm water for 2 minutes.

Put each vine leaf shiny (top) side down and place a sardine on it. Roll up so that just the head and tail are seen. Brush the leaves all over with olive oil and grill on a barbecue for about 5 minutes each side.

Serve in the vine leaves with lemon wedges on the side.

GRILLED SEABASS
WITH BLITVA GREENS

This comes from the island of Korčula in Croatia. The fish was superb, but it was the accompanying potato and bean dish called blitva that especially caught my attention. It's one of those side dishes that you find yourself making over and over again; nothing surprising about it – it is just lovely.

SERVES SIX

8 medium potatoes,
   peeled and cut into
   large chunks
800g French beans,
   trimmed and cut in half
15g/3 cloves garlic,
   crushed or grated
60ml olive oil, plus extra
   for brushing
Salt and freshly ground
   black pepper
6 seabass or seabream fillets

Boil the potatoes in salted water until just tender. Boil the French beans for 6 minutes until cooked, not just al dente but quite soft. Drain each and reserve some of the cooking liquid.

Fry the garlic gently in the olive oil until softened, then add the well-drained potato chunks and French beans, season with salt and pepper and cook for 1 minute, mixing well together. The potatoes will break up a little but that's what you want.

Brush the fish fillets with a little olive oil and grill over high heat for 3 minutes. Serve the fish with the blitva alongside. If you prefer your blitva a little soupy, add some of the reserved cooking liquid.

JOHN DORY ALLA CARLINA

When people ask me, 'Where is your favourite restaurant in the world?', I reply,
'It depends how I am feeling.' If you are in love, shall we say desperately in love, it has
to be Locanda Cipriani on the Venetian island of Torcello on a crisp winter's lunchtime.
You arrive reclining in a vaporetto with a view just skimming the water. You see the low
islands of Murano, Burano and Torcello. You go into Torcello cathedral and see the
fabulous Byzantine mosaic of the Last Judgement. You are probably thinking of
Hemingway and how he used to stay at Locanda Cipriani when he was duck shooting,
and once persuaded them to keep it open all winter just for him. The sharp bright
coldness gives you an appetite for lunch. You walk in and there is a log fire blazing and
you sit down and order cicchetti and this John Dory dish … You will probably also want
a glass or two of pinot grigio, such as Tiefenbrunner from Alto Adige in the Tyrol.

SERVES FOUR

4 John Dory fillets
  (ask the fishmonger
  for the bones to make
  the stock)
Salt and freshly ground
  black pepper
50g plain flour
2 tbsp olive oil,
  plus extra to serve
1 lemon, halved
1 tsp Worcestershire sauce
2 small gherkins,
  finely chopped
2 tbsp capers: 1 tbsp finely
  chopped, 1 tbsp whole
2 tomatoes, peeled, deseeded
  and finely chopped
3 tbsp *Tomato sauce* (page 307)
250ml *Fish stock* (page 308)
Small handful flat-leaf
  parsley, chopped

Season the John Dory fillets with some salt and pepper
and lightly dust with flour. Heat the olive oil in a frying
pan, add the fillets skin-side down and fry for 2–3 minutes
until lightly browned, then season with a squeeze of lemon
juice, turn the fish over and cook for a further minute.
Remove from the pan and keep warm.

Add the Worcestershire sauce, gherkins, whole and
chopped capers, tomatoes, tomato sauce and fish stock
to the pan, bring to the boil then reduce a little to create
the sauce. Add the fish carefully back to the pan for
a minute to warm through in the sauce.

Serve immediately, drizzled with a little more olive
oil and sprinkled with fresh parsley.

BAKED TURBOT WITH POTATOES & VEGETABLES
Rombo al forno con patate e verdure

I probably go on a bit too much about the simplicity of Venetian seafood cookery, but for me, just as my first visit to Goa in India in the 1980s expanded my horizons into fish curries, so a visit in the early 1980s to Venice influenced many dishes I subsequently put on my menu: warm shellfish, crab with linguine, pasta alle vongole, to name a few. This turbot from the island of Pellestrina, just next to the Lido, is another fabulously simple dish. I had lunch there with Skye McAlpine, daughter of my late and much missed friend Alistair, who shares her father's articulate love of simple cooking.

SERVES FOUR

1kg whole turbot, skin on
400g potatoes, peeled and
    sliced 5mm thick
Salt and freshly ground
    black pepper
1 aubergine
2 courgettes
4 artichoke hearts, freshly
    trimmed or from a jar
7 cherry tomatoes
100ml white wine
Small handful flat-leaf
    parsley, chopped

For the infused oil
100ml olive oil
1 small onion, halved
    and sliced
1 sprig thyme
1 sprig rosemary
3 sage leaves
2 bay leaves
50ml white wine
½ tsp salt
5 turns black peppermill

Make the infused oil by simmering all the ingredients in a pan for 20–30 minutes. Turn off the heat and leave for 15 minutes, then strain.

To prepare the turbot, cut through the dark skin all the way round the fish, close to the frill-like fins.

Heat 60ml of the infused oil in a pan, add the sliced potatoes and fry for 8–10 minutes until golden. Season and set aside.

Cut the aubergine lengthways into 8 slices, then across into 5cm strips. Cut the courgettes lengthways in half, then across into strips as for the aubergine. Quarter the artichoke hearts. Halve the cherry tomatoes.

Heat the oven to 190°C/gas 5. Pour half the remaining infused oil into an ovenproof dish along with the white wine. Lay the turbot white-side down on one side of the dish. On the other side of the dish put the vegetables, season with salt and pepper and drizzle with the remaining infused oil. Bake for 18 minutes.

Transfer the fish to a warmed serving dish and carefully remove the top skin. Remove portion-sized pieces of the top fillets by sliding a palette knife under and lifting them off the bones. Then lift off the bones to give you access to the two bottom fillets. Serve sprinkled with chopped parsley, with the vegetables alongside.

GREEK FISH STEW

This is not exactly the same recipe as the chef at the Poseidon restaurant, Panagiotis, cooked for me that day because I like to put my own little spin on things, but in essence it is. What I enjoy about fish stews in Greece is that they are no big deal. We are not talking bouillabaisse, zarzuela or cacciucco, just a local fish stew to be accompanied by a local Greek salad and some increasingly good, local, chilled white wine – though I still have an affection for retsina.

SERVES FOUR

75ml olive oil
1 bulb fennel, diced
2 carrots, diced
1 red onion, diced
10g/2 cloves garlic,
    finely chopped
1 large tomato, diced
200g new potatoes,
    scrubbed and halved
Leaves from 1 celery head
1 litre *Fish stock* (page 308)
50ml ouzo (or pastis)
Large pinch saffron strands
1 tsp salt
15 turns black peppermill
½ tsp chilli flakes
250g seabass (2 fillets)
250g bream (2 fillets)
8 raw prawns, shelled
1 lemon, halved

Heat the olive oil in a pan over a medium heat, add the fennel, carrot and onion, and fry for 3–5 minutes until starting to soften. Then add the garlic and fry for 1–2 minutes more.

Add the tomato, potato, celery leaves, fish stock and ouzo and bring to the boil. Reduce the heat, add the saffron, salt, pepper and chilli flakes, and simmer for 10 minutes.

Add the fish, skin-side up, and cook for about 10 minutes, uncovered. Add the prawns and heat through for 2 minutes, squeeze over the lemon juice and serve.

MESUT'S BLUE FISH STEW WITH CHILLI CORNBREAD

Mesut is a very pleasant fisherman who works the Bosphorus in his small diesel engine boat, dodging the steady procession of oil tankers and passenger liners. When the crew were filming me fishing with him, they said it looked as if the boat was in danger of capsizing from the wash, but I was too absorbed in the fishing to notice. I wish we had blue fish in the UK; fortunately for me, however, in my other home in Sydney they do, known there as trevally. Similar to mackerel but with a creamy taste, blue fish are loved by the Turks, especially the new season ones we were fishing for that day. This is a common dish in Turkey. I had another one made with bream, but it is much better with a more flavoursome fish like this. In Turkey they serve it with cornbread; the recipe below comes from Leith's cookery school and is made with jalapeño chillies and coriander.

SERVES FOUR

4 small mackerel or herring,
    scaled and gutted
1 tsp salt
100ml olive oil
1 onion, halved and sliced
6 green finger chillies,
    split open but kept whole
Large handful
    flat-leaf parsley
12 turns black peppermill
3 tomatoes, peeled
    and chopped
30g/6 cloves garlic, sliced
1 lemon, skin and pith
    removed, sliced

For the chilli cornbread
200g plain flour
70g yellow cornmeal
1 tbsp baking powder
Pinch salt
4 tbsp chopped coriander
2–3 jalapeño chillies, deseeded
    and finely chopped
50g feta cheese, crumbled
30g soft light brown sugar
6 tbsp water
3 large eggs
70ml sunflower oil

To make the cornbread, first heat the oven to 180°C/gas 4 and warm a baking sheet. Place paper cases in a 12-hole muffin tin.

Sift the flour, cornmeal, baking powder and salt into a large bowl. Stir in the coriander, chillies, feta and sugar.

In a jug, mix together the water, eggs and oil. Add to the dry ingredients and mix together until just combined. Fill each paper case about two-thirds full, then sit the tin on the warmed baking sheet.

Bake for 15–20 minutes or until a sharp knife inserted into the centre comes out clean. Allow the cornbread buns to cool in the tin for 5 minutes.

While the cornbread is baking, sprinkle the fish with the salt inside and out.

Pour 2 tablespoons of the olive oil into a large pan with a lid, scatter the onions in the base and lay the fish on top. Tuck the chillies and sprigs of parsley in around the fish and sprinkle with the pepper. Add the tomatoes, garlic and slices of lemon, and pour the remaining olive oil over the top. Cover the pan with the lid, bring to a simmer and cook on a medium heat for about 25 minutes. Serve with warm cornbread.

GNOCCHI CON GRANSEOLA

A classic Venetian dish, granseola is actually spider crab meat. This is hard to come by so do feel free to use white crab meat instead. The flavour that makes this dish for me is the Byzantine spice mix (see page 307).

SERVES FOUR

For the gnocchi
225g floury potatoes
    in their skins
80g plain flour
Salt
½ egg, beaten (20g)

For the crab sauce
75ml olive oil
½ small onion, grated
5g/1 clove garlic, grated
Pinch chilli flakes
¼ tsp *Byzantine spice mix*
    (page 307)
300ml prawn stock
    (see *Petros's clams*, page 73)
20g butter
Small handful flat-leaf
    parsley, finely chopped
200g white crab meat

For the gnocchi, first heat the oven to 180°C/gas 4. Bake the potatoes for 50 minutes until very soft, then leave to cool. Scoop the flesh from the skins and mash it or pass through a potato ricer. Mix it with the flour, ¼ teaspoon of salt and the egg to make a firm dough.

Roll the mixture into 1cm-thick sausages, then cut into 2cm lengths. Boil in salted water for 3 minutes, until they rise to the surface, while you start to make the sauce. When cooked, drain and keep warm while you finish the sauce.

Heat the olive oil in a pan over a medium heat and sweat the onion and garlic for 5 minutes until soft, then add the chilli flakes and spice mix and stir for 1 minute. Add the prawn stock, bring to a simmer to reduce down a little, then whisk in the knob of butter. Fold in the parsley and crab meat and pour over the cooked gnocchi.

BUTRINT MUSSELS

Butrint is opposite the Greek island of Corfu and is surrounded by an estuary, ideal for growing mussels. I was there with my son Jack, on my last day in Albania, watching the chef prepare this dish. Rather ignorantly, we were disdainful of cooking shellfish with a fair amount of feta cheese in it. I suppose we were indoctrinated by the Italian refusal to pair cheese with any seafood. Almost inevitably, when we came to taste the dish of steaming mussels, it was delicious.

SERVES TWO

60ml olive oil
1 small onion,
  halved and sliced
5g/1 clove garlic, sliced
1 smallish green pepper,
  deseeded and sliced
30ml ouzo (or pastis)
600g mussels, in the
  shell, scrubbed
150ml passata
75g feta cheese
½ tsp chilli flakes
½ tsp salt
Freshly ground black pepper
Small handful fennel herb
  or dill, chopped

Heat the olive oil in a large pan over a medium heat and sweat the onion, garlic and green pepper for 5 minutes.

Add the ouzo and the mussels, cover with a lid and cook for about 5 minutes until the mussels start to open. Discard any that don't open.

Add the passata and feta and season with the chilli flakes, salt and some black pepper. Heat through for 1–2 minutes and serve scattered with fennel herb or dill.

BIGOLI IN SALSA

I keep picking up advice about Venetian cooking that it is very basic and not particularly inspired. This dish is rather indicative of that sentiment in that it looks pretty dull – just pasta with onions and a bit of anchovy. In fact, it is now one of my favourite pasta dishes ever. It demonstrates how understated, but how incredibly good, the cooking of Venice is. Try it and you will see what I mean. Incidentally, I have retained the name 'bigoli', which is a solid, thick, spaghetti-like pasta, although it is virtually impossible to get outside of Venice. Bucatini, the same size but hollow in the middle, is what I use.

SERVES FOUR

250g bucatini pasta
Salt
60ml olive oil,
    plus extra to serve
1 large onion,
    finely chopped
5g/1 clove garlic,
    finely chopped
8 tinned anchovy fillets
250ml *Chicken stock*
    (page 307)
10 turns black peppermill
Small bunch flat-leaf
    parsley, chopped

Bring a large pot of salted water to the boil for the pasta.

Heat the olive oil in a large frying pan over a medium heat, add the onion and garlic and cook slowly for 10–15 minutes until very soft. Add the anchovies, breaking them up a little with a wooden spoon, then add the chicken stock and simmer until two-thirds of the liquid has evaporated. Taste, season with ½ teaspoon of salt (if needed) and the black pepper, and keep warm in the pan.

Cook the bucatini for 10 minutes or until al dente, drain and add to the sauce in the pan. Stir through three-quarters of the parsley and serve, sprinkled with the remaining parsley and a drizzle of olive oil.

BIGOLI IN CASSOPIPA

The Agopyan family have been running the Antiche Carampane restaurant for the last thirty years. Every morning they can be seen sat around a table with their staff, cleaning fish and shellfish bought minutes earlier in the market. Other than fish, they also serve liver and onions. I was taken there by Francesco da Mosto, whose BBC series on Venice I really enjoyed. I liked him a lot and probably told him how well dressed he was. How is it that Italians, even when they are wearing the most casual gear, in his case jeans and scuffed loafers, seem to have the exact jacket you want? I have used the spice blend that is the trade mark of this excellent pasta dish in another dish, too: the gnocchi con granseola on page 226.

SERVES SIX

400g mussels, in the
   shell, scrubbed
90ml olive oil,
   plus extra to serve
1 small onion, finely chopped
1 carrot, finely grated
1 stick celery, finely grated
1 small leek, finely chopped
2 tsp *Byzantine spice mix*
   (page 307)
100ml white wine
300ml *Fish* or *Chicken stock*
   (page 307)
Salt
400g bucatini or spaghetti
300g raw prawns,
   heads removed
8 scallops, halved horizontally
250g squid rings and tentacles
1 tbsp tomato paste
Small handful flat-leaf
   parsley, roughly chopped

Steam the mussels with a splash of water in a large lidded pan over a high heat for about 4 minutes until open, then remove the meat from the shells and set aside, along with the cooking liquor.

In a large pan over a medium heat, heat 3 tablespoons of the olive oil. Add the onion, carrot, celery and leek, cover with a lid and cook for about 10 minutes. Add the spice mix and fry for 1–2 minutes. Add the white wine, stock, 1 teaspoon of salt and the mussel liquor, and bring up to a simmer. Cook until most of the liquid has evaporated.

Cook the pasta in plenty of salted boiling water for 10 minutes or until al dente.

Just before the pasta is ready, in a separate frying pan, fry the prawns, scallops and squid in the remaining olive oil (3 tablespoons). Stir in the tomato paste, then combine with the fried vegetables and the previously cooked mussels.

Drain the pasta, add to seafood sauce and mix well. Serve drizzled with olive oil and chopped parsley.

SPAGHETTI WITH CLAMS & BOTTARGA

Finding good places to eat in Venice is not always about somewhere at the end of a long canal. The Hotel Wildner is right by the San Zaccaria vaporetto stop near St Mark's Square. It's family owned and run, and the son, Luca Fullin, made this classic vongole dish for us. The apple of his mum's eye, so it seemed to me, full of enthusiasm and good humour, he made this with the triangular-shaped clams called telline that aren't actually from the lagoon but the Adriatic. They were tiny and exquisitely sweet. Small vongole (palourdes, carpetshell clams) would be almost as good. The other house speciality was that he prepared it with a bottarga made from bass roe; ordinary bottarga made with the roe of the grey mullet would be equally good. If you want to make this in Australia, pippies would be the nearest thing to telline.

SERVES FOUR

300g spaghetti
Salt and white pepper
4 tbsp olive oil
10g/2 cloves garlic,
    crushed or grated
2 tbsp dry white wine
250g small clams
Small bunch flat-leaf
    parsley, chopped
Small bunch of
    chives, chopped
15g bottarga

Cook the spaghetti in plenty of salted boiling water for 10 minutes or until al dente.

While the pasta is cooking, slowly heat the oil with the crushed garlic in a large, heavy-based pan, then add the white wine.

When the spaghetti is almost ready, add the clams to the wine, cover the pan with a lid and steam over a high heat for 2 minutes until the shells open. (Discard any that don't open.)

Drain the spaghetti when al dente and add to the clams, stirring to coat the pasta with the liquor from the clams.

Serve in a bowl sprinkle liberally with chopped parsley, chives and a little white pepper. Finish by grating over bottarga.

SPAGHETTINI WITH SLIPPER LOBSTER

Slipper lobsters are the same sort of crustacean as Australian Balmain bugs, and make very good eating. I went out with a couple of divers who were picking them from the rocks near the fishing village of Limeni. We came back and the very pretty wife of one of them, called Dimitra, cooked them in her restaurant kitchen while her aunt hovered over the whole procedure with a critical eye. There was no doubt in my mind whose kitchen this really was. There is nothing much to this dish, and I think it would be a good way to serve our own lobster too.

SERVES TWO

1 lobster (about 800g)
Salt for cooking
100ml olive oil
3 beefsteak tomatoes, peeled and chopped
1 onion, finely chopped
1 tbsp tomato paste
1 red long or bell pepper, deseeded and sliced 1cm thick
½ tsp sea salt
170g spaghettini
A few leaves of fresh basil, thinly sliced

Freeze the raw lobster for 2 hours prior to cooking. Bring a large pan of water to the boil, salt it well (1 tsp salt to every 600ml water) and cook the lobster for 15–20 minutes, depending on size. When cooked, remove from the water, cut in half lengthways and set aside, reserving the water you cooked it in.

In a separate pan, heat the olive oil and add the tomatoes, onion, tomato paste, red pepper and sea salt, and cook for 10 minutes over a medium heat. Add 500ml of the lobster cooking liquid and the spaghettini. Cook for 10 minutes or until the spaghettini is al dente. Add the basil leaves and lobster to the pan and warm the lobster through for about 3 minutes.

Serve in a large bowl with the spaghettini in the middle and the lobster halves either side.

SEAFOOD LINGUINE

The seafood town of Vlorë is probably the best place to visit in Albania for those wanting the pleasures of the Mediterranean coastline. The Paradise Beach Hotel is just outside: good swimming I have to say, and lovely seafood. This is, of course, an Italian dish, but I didn't think it suffered at all by being made by a very engaging Albanian chef by the sea.

SERVES FOUR

60ml olive oil
10g/2 cloves garlic, crushed, no need to peel
12 medium raw prawns, peeled, shells and heads reserved
2 tbsp tomato paste
300ml water
350g linguine
Salt
60g squid rings and tentacles
16 mussels, in the shell, scrubbed
¼ tsp chilli flakes
2 handfuls cherry tomatoes, halved
10 turns black peppermill
Handful of flat-leaf parsley, roughly chopped

Heat half the olive oil in a pan, add the garlic and prawn heads and shells and fry over a high heat for 5 minutes, turning them from time to time. Add the tomato paste and water, simmer with the lid on for 10 minutes, then use a stick blender to blitz the mixture. Pass through a sieve and reserve.

Cook the linguine in plenty of salted boiling water for 10 minutes or until al dente.

Wipe out the pan then add the rest of the olive oil and fry the squid and prawns over a high heat for 2 minutes. Add the strained prawn and tomato stock, then the mussels, chilli flakes and cherry tomatoes. Bring to the boil with the lid on and boil rapidly for 4 minutes until the mussels have opened. (Discard any that don't open.) Remove the lid and if necessary reduce the liquor to a sauce consistency, then season with ½ teaspoon of salt and the pepper. Add the well-drained pasta along with the parsley and toss together well. Serve immediately.

LINGUINE WITH COURGETTES & BOTTARGA

I had heard of Messolonghi as where bottarga is made, years before I went there. The town is surrounded by lagoons perfect for trapping grey mullet for their roe, which is cured with salt and allowed to dry. I must confess to becoming a bit of a bottarga addict, with some damage to my pocket. The last lot I bought was £190 per kilogram. I hasten to add, I bought only 75g! Short of thinly slicing it and eating it just like that, or maybe with some sourdough bread, the best way of serving it up is in a very simple pasta dish like this. Petros Paragios, who looked after us in Messolonghi, makes excellent bottarga. It's a small world: I can buy his bottarga, called Stefos, at the Chelsea fishmonger just down the road from my London flat, and his brother Kostas sorted out our wonderful harbourside villa in Symi where we filmed so many of the dishes in this book.

SERVES FOUR

400g linguine
Salt and freshly ground
    black pepper
3 tbsp olive oil,
    plus extra to serve
10g/2 cloves garlic,
    finely chopped
¼ tsp chilli flakes
300g courgettes, cut into
    fine 3cm-long batons
Small handful flat-leaf
    parsley, chopped
1 lemon, halved
15g bottarga

Cook the linguine in plenty of salted boiling water for about 8 minutes or until al dente.

Just before the pasta is ready, heat the olive oil in a frying pan over a medium heat and add the garlic, chilli flakes and courgettes. Cook for 4 minutes until starting to soften, then remove from the heat and season with salt and pepper.

Drain the pasta well and mix with the garlicky courgettes. Add the parsley, drizzle with a little more olive oil and squeeze over some lemon juice. Serve immediately, with the finely grated bottarga on top, rather as you would serve Parmesan.

SEAFOOD RISOTTO

I have written recipes for seafood risotto before but never made it with the distinctive mix of spices so particular to Venice, which I call a Byzantine spice mix. We had a really good guide there called Christina Pigozzo, very articulate and committed to all things Venetian, particularly the cooking. I asked her what dish would she miss the most if she were forced to leave Venice, never to return. This is it. As with all my mixed seafood dishes, the ingredients are only what I would like. Feel free to use whatever you do.

SERVES FOUR

60ml olive oil
2 shallots, finely chopped
5g/1 clove garlic, grated
350g Arborio or
    Carnaroli rice
¼ tsp *Byzantine spice mix*
    (page 307)
125ml dry white wine
1.5 litres *Fish stock*
    (page 308), hot
8 mussels, in the
    shell, scrubbed
150ml prawn stock:
    see *Petros's clams*
    (page 73), hot
2 red mullet fillets, cut
    diagonally into strips
1 squid, cleaned and cut
    into rings, plus tentacles
100g small shrimps,
    preferably raw
½ tsp salt
6 turns black peppermill
30g butter
100g white crab meat
Small handful flat-leaf
    parsley, chopped

In a large sauté pan over a medium heat, warm 3 tablespoons of the olive oil and fry the shallots and garlic gently until softened. Add the rice and fry it in the oil for 2 minutes, then add the spice mix and stir it through the rice.

Add the white wine, bring to a simmer and allow it to evaporate, then stir in a ladle of hot fish stock. When this has been absorbed, add the next ladle, and continue to do so, stirring after each addition, until you have only a couple of ladlefuls left –16–18 minutes. Add the mussels and prawn stock.

Heat the remaining tablespoon of olive oil in a frying pan until simmering and fry the red mullet strips, squid rings and tentacles and shrimps briskly for 2–3 minutes. Season with the salt and pepper. Stir the seafood into the risotto with the remaining fish stock and cook for 1–2 minutes until absorbed. Stir in the butter, crab meat and parsley, and serve at once.

BLACK RISOTTO

I do find it a bit dreary that, when talking to the media about a book and series like this, the inevitable question is, 'What is your favourite dish?' But I have to admit it is not an unreasonable one, and the answer is this cuttlefish risotto. As I said on page 311, what makes it so special is that the cuttlefish is of such good quality, and also that they use about twice as much cuttlefish ink as I have ever seen in a printed recipe. Before someone complains about me putting Parmesan in an Italian seafood dish, this was Croatia, not Italy, and they did, and it's very good.

SERVES FOUR TO SIX

400g prepared cuttlefish
90ml olive oil,
    plus extra to serve
1 small shallot, chopped
10g/2 cloves garlic, chopped
350g Arborio or Carnaroli
    rice, rinsed
100ml white wine
1.2 litre *Fish stock*
    (page 308), hot
4 x 4g cuttlefish ink sachets
1 tbsp freshly grated
    Parmesan cheese
Salt and freshly ground
    black pepper
30g butter
Small handful flat-leaf
    parsley, chopped

Separate the tentacles of the cuttlefish, set aside, and cut the body into 1cm squares.

Heat the olive oil in a large frying pan over a high heat and sauté the cuttlefish, both body and tentacles, for 2 minutes. Reduce the heat a little, then add the shallot and garlic and cook for 2 minutes to soften.

Add the rice and toast it in the oil for 2 minutes, then add the white wine. Bring to a simmer to allow this to evaporate before adding the first ladle of hot fish stock. When this has been absorbed, add the next ladle, and so on, stirring after each addition, until nearly all the stock has been absorbed and the rice is cooked – 15–16 minutes. At this point add the sachets of ink to the pan.

Season with the grated Parmesan and some salt and pepper, and stir in the butter. Serve drizzled with a little olive oil and sprinkled with chopped parsley.

★★★★★★ VEGETARIAN & SIDES

*I would go as far as to say that vegetable dishes are
the most important part of the Mediterranean diet.*

I could write the whole introduction to this chapter about one dish:
Green beans in tomato sauce, *fasulye* in Turkish, *fasolakia* in Greek,
on page 261.

I used to go to Greece every year in the late 1960s. The food was
not always great, as anyone from my generation will attest, but the
one thing that was always perfect was green beans in tomato sauce.
The wonderful thing about this dish is the more you cook it, the better
it gets. These days we like peas or beans very briefly cooked, but there
is something incredibly comforting when the beans have become
almost khaki coloured and have a stewed flavour. To me, *fasolakia* in
Greece is like rice in Southeast Asia: a must with every meal. But it
is also one of a lexicon of vegetable dishes in that part of the world
that can be eaten without any thought of meat.

I would go as far as to say that vegetable dishes are the most
important part of the Mediterranean diet. They come from hitherto
poor parts of the world, and necessity is always the mother of invention.
Indeed, some of the best vegetarian recipes in Greece come from Greek
Orthodox Lent, when meat and fish is forbidden. But it is not just
Greece and Turkey. If you look at a lot of great Italian food, it is also
vegetarian. Take the spinach and ricotta ravioli with wild mushroom
sauté on page 251, for example. It seems to me to sum up everything
that is so special about Italian cuisine: a deft touch here and there,
in this case the harmonious mix of spinach and ricotta in the ravioli,
but then the subtle taste of nutmeg, too, and a sauce of delicious
autumnal mushrooms finished with Parmesan and sage leaves.

RISOTTO ALLA TORCELLANA

This is Locanda Cipriani's very stylized version of risotto primavera, which is risotto with spring vegetables. I confess to having changed it quite a lot, simply because the dish as we filmed it is the product of a large and very capable kitchen, able to produce lots of different vegetables to go in it. I have cut these right down, but I hope I have kept the essence of it. Certainly I have included the artichoke hearts – a lovely memory for me of a market garden growing them just across the canal from the restaurant.

SERVES SIX

2 tbsp olive oil,
  plus extra to serve
1 small leek, finely chopped
2 small courgettes,
  finely chopped
200g fine green beans,
  trimmed and cut
  into 2cm lengths
Handful wild garlic leaves,
  chopped, or 1 large clove
  garlic, crushed or grated
450g Arborio or
  Carnaroli rice
1.8 litres *Vegetable stock*
  (page 307), hot
4 artichoke hearts, freshly
  trimmed, or from a jar
200g fresh green peas
6 asparagus spears
40g butter, diced
75g Parmesan cheese,
  finely grated
1 tsp salt
12 turns black peppermill
Small handful flat-leaf
  parsley, chopped

In a large frying pan over a medium heat, warm the olive oil and add the leek, courgettes, green beans and crushed garlic if using. Cook for 2–3 minutes until just softened, then add the rice and stir to heat through and coat in the olive oil.

Add a ladle of hot stock and stir until absorbed. Continue to add the stock, a ladle at a time, stirring until it has been absorbed, for another 10 minutes, then add the artichoke hearts, peas and asparagus. Continue to add the hot stock until the rice is just cooked, which should be about another 8 minutes.

Remove from the heat and stir in the butter, wild garlic, if using, and Parmesan, and season with the salt and pepper. Serve sprinkled with parsley and with a drizzle of olive oil.

TURKISH COURGETTE & CARROT FRITTERS

The Turks love their fritters. They seem to take any vegetables in season and mix them with herbs and spices to produce something delightful as part of a mezze. There are two recipes here: one with grated courgettes and one with grated carrots. They are particularly good served with cacık (yogurt, garlic and cucumber dip with mint and dill, page 35).

MAKES ABOUT TWENTY OF EACH

Sunflower oil, for
  shallow frying
Cacık (page 35), to serve

For the courgette fritters
3 medium courgettes, grated
1½ tsp salt
15g/3 cloves garlic,
  finely chopped
½ onion, finely chopped
3 spring onions, sliced
3 eggs, beaten
150g white brined cheese,
  such as feta, crumbled
1 tsp fennel seeds
Small handful fennel
  herb, chopped
Pinch chilli flakes
8 turns black peppermill
5–6 tbsp plain flour

For the carrot fritters
3 large carrots, grated and
  dried on kitchen paper
5g/1 clove garlic, chopped
¼ onion, finely chopped
3 spring onions, sliced
3 eggs, beaten
Small handful dill, chopped
1 tsp cumin seeds
Pinch chilli flakes
½ tsp salt
8 turns black peppermill
5–6 tbsp plain flour

For the courgette fritters, put the grated courgette in a colander, sprinkle with a teaspoon of the salt and leave for 20 minutes. Rinse, then squeeze in a clean tea towel to extract as much liquid as possible.

In a large bowl, combine all the ingredients for the kind of fritter you are making. Increase the amount of flour slightly if the mixture is too wet.

Heat a little oil in a frying pan. When hot, add spoonfuls of the batter and flatten slightly with the back of a spoon. Cook over a medium heat until golden brown, 3–4 minutes, then turn over and repeat. Drain on kitchen paper and keep warm while you make the rest. Serve warm or cold.

SPINACH & RICOTTA RAVIOLI WITH WILD MUSHROOM SAUTÉ

The idea from this came from Harry's Bar in Venice. I thought it was such an intelligent way of serving seasonal wild mushrooms: a simple ravioli stuffed with spinach and ricotta and flavoured with nutmeg, with sautéed wild mushrooms scattered on top.
Recipe photograph overleaf

SERVES SIX

For the pasta
300g 00 pasta flour,
    plus extra for dusting
1 tsp salt
3 eggs, beaten,
    plus 1 for sealing

For the filling
1.5kg fresh spinach
500g ricotta cheese
2 eggs, beaten
1 tsp salt
6 turns black peppermill
Pinch freshly grated nutmeg

To finish
Salt
30g butter
4 large handfuls fresh
    wild mushrooms,
    such as chanterelles,
    oyster, porcini
Handful small sage leaves
70g freshly grated Parmesan
Black peppermill

Mix the flour, salt and eggs to 'breadcrumbs' in a food processor, then tip on to a lightly floured surface and bring together to form a dough. Knead for 3–4 minutes until smooth and elastic. Wrap in cling film and leave to rest for half an hour before rolling, while you make the filling.

Wash the spinach and wilt it quickly over a high heat in just the water that clings to the leaves after washing. Drain, then squeeze between 2 plates to get rid of as much water as possible. Chop the spinach well and mix with the ricotta cheese and eggs. Season with the salt, pepper and nutmeg.

Divide the pasta into 2 pieces and roll each into a 2mm-thick, long sheet, using a rolling pin or with a pasta machine. Lay on a lightly floured surface. Dot teaspoonfuls of the ricotta mixture at intervals along one pasta sheet. Brush between the filling and along the edges of the pasta with beaten egg, place the other sheet on top, press down around the filling, then, using a knife or pizza cutter, cut out ravioli about 5cm square.

Boil the pasta in a large pan of salted water for 4–5 minutes, then drain.

While the pasta is cooking, heat the butter in a frying pan over a high heat and sauté the wild mushrooms with the sage leaves for 1–2 minutes. Serve the ravioli sprinkled with Parmesan and topped with mushrooms, and grind some black pepper over.

HORTA PIE
Hortopita

In a lot of Mediterranean countries the gathering of wild greens is part of life.
I have filmed excursions in Italy and Greece before and asked the simple question,
'Why don't we do this back home?' There is plenty to choose from: nettles, wild
parsley, purslane, sea kale, dandelions and wild garlic to name but a few. However,
this pie is also well worth making with leaves you can buy, such as chard,
spinach, radicchio or rocket.

SERVES FOUR

10 sheets filo pastry
Olive oil, for greasing
   and brushing

For the filling
1.5kg horta (mixed greens):
   such as dandelion leaves,
   wild garlic, nettles,
   chard, spinach
2 medium or 3 small
   onions, halved and sliced
2 eggs
300g feta cheese, crumbled
1 tsp salt
20 turns black peppermill

To prepare the filling, wash and chop the horta. In a large
bowl, combine the onions with the eggs, then add the horta
and feta and mix well. Season with the salt and pepper.

Heat the oven to 180°C/gas 4. Oil the base of a 40–45cm
ovenproof dish, then line with a sheet of filo pastry. Brush
with olive oil, then place another sheet on top. Continue
until you have 5 sheets of the filo in the dish. Put the horta
mixture in the dish. Place the remaining 5 sheets of filo on
top, oiling between each layer. Fold in the pastry from the
edges to seal the filling in the pie, brush the top with more
olive oil and bake for 10 minutes.

Remove from the oven, cut into quarters (to enable
the pastry to dry out) and return to the oven for a further
50 minutes. The pie is now ready to serve. It is delicious
served warm or cold.

GREEK SALAD

Why bother with a recipe for the ubiquitous Greek salad? Well, there are some subtleties to it that need to be observed. First, the herb. Some prefer dill, some oregano. Everywhere I went on this trip it was oregano, and not just any old oregano but bags of the dried stuff brought down from the hills. Secondly, the feta: crumble or slab? The nicest salads, I think, come with a few slabs of feta on top, which you then break into your serving. Lastly, dressed with lemon juice or vinegar? The fact that in Greek tavernas you usually get bottles of vinegar and olive oil seems to suggest vinegar. I have written a recipe based on 4 parts oil to 1 part vinegar. As the saying goes, I like to be mean with the vinegar and profligate with the olive oil. *Recipe photograph overleaf*

SERVES FOUR

450g ripe red well-
    flavoured tomatoes
½ cucumber
1 red onion
20 black olives
4 tbsp olive oil,
    plus extra to serve
1 tbsp red wine vinegar
½ tsp salt
6 turns black peppermill
1 tsp dried oregano
200g feta cheese

Cut the tomatoes into chunks. Cut the cucumber in half lengthways and then into thick slices. Slice the red onion very thinly. Put into a large serving bowl with the olives.

Make a dressing by mixing together the olive oil, vinegar, salt and pepper. Pour over the salad. Slice the feta, place on top and sprinkle with the dried oregano. Drizzle with a little more olive oil and serve at once.

STUFFED VEGETABLES

When we were filming in Greece, stuffed vegetables was our favourite dish. It all stemmed from a brief stop-off for lunch when driving from Preveza to Messolonghi. We called in at the little fishing village of Astakos, which means something like 'lobster village', stopped at the first quayside café we came to and asked what was for lunch. They said stuffed tomatoes and peppers, which had just come out of the oven. The Greeks say they prefer their vegetables lukewarm, having had some time to rest after cooking. But my memory of stuffed vegetables from the 1970s is that they were cold, and not great. This may have had something to do with the fact that in those days, after plenty of retsina, we were not early risers. Straight from the oven when you are ravenously hungry is perfect: as David says about once every three days, 'This is the best thing I have ever eaten.'

SERVES EIGHT TO TEN

1 each green, red
  and yellow pepper
2 large tomatoes
2 small–medium aubergines
1 each medium green
  and yellow courgette
6 tbsp olive oil
1 large onion, finely chopped
10g/2 cloves garlic,
  finely chopped
2½ tbsp tomato paste
400g long-grain rice, rinsed
250ml *Vegetable stock*
  (page 307)
2 tsp salt
12 turns black peppermill
Large handful
  flat-leaf parsley
Large handful fresh mint
1 tsp dried oregano
⅛ tsp chilli flakes

Prepare the vegetables for stuffing. Cut the tops off the peppers and tomatoes to create a lid and set aside. Scoop out the pepper seeds and discard. Scoop out the tomato flesh and seeds and reserve. Cut the aubergines and courgettes lengthways and scoop out the seeds and flesh inside, leaving a boat-shaped shell ready to fill. Add the flesh from the courgettes and aubergines to the tomato flesh and seeds and chop well.

In a large pan over a medium heat, warm 3 tablespoons of the olive oil and fry the onion and garlic for 3–5 minutes until soft, then add the chopped vegetable flesh and the tomato paste. Cook for about 10 minutes until softened. Add the rice and 150ml of the vegetable stock, raise to a simmer and and cook for 10 minutes, stirring occasionally. (The rice will continue to cook in the oven.) Season with the salt and pepper and stir in the herbs and chilli flakes.

Heat the oven to 160°C/gas 3. Arrange the vegetable shells in a roasting tin or ovenproof dish and spoon the rice mixture into them. Place the lids on the peppers and tomatoes and drizzle them all with the remaining olive oil. Pour the remaining stock into the tin, cover with foil and bake for 1 hour, then remove the foil and bake for another 15–30 minutes until the vegetables and rice are cooked. Serve hot, warm or cold.

BANDIT'S JOY

I was intrigued by this Albanian recipe from *Round the World in Eighty Dishes* by the late Lesley Blanch. Would it work, potatoes with honey? It did. This really is extraordinarily good.

SERVES FOUR

4 large sweet potatoes
    (or regular potatoes)
Salt and freshly ground
    black pepper
2 tbsp butter
Nutmeg
Lemon half
100ml clear honey

Parboil the potatoes in their skins in salted water for about 5 minutes. When cool enough to handle, peel and cut into thick, chunky slices.

In a large frying pan, melt the butter and fry the potatoes until lightly golden, then grate over some nutmeg, squeeze over some lemon juice and drizzle with the honey. Season with 1 teaspoon of salt and pepper to taste. Serve at once.

GREEN BEANS IN TOMATO SAUCE
Taze fasulye

This is the Turkish version of the same Greek dish I always seem to order. Don't be afraid to let the beans stew for a long time. The flavour improves as they lose their fresh greenness and turn khaki. You can use runner beans, or pulses like butterbeans, too.

SERVES SIX

8 tbsp olive oil
1 small onion, chopped
10g/2 cloves garlic, crushed or grated
5 medium tomatoes, chopped
1 tbsp tomato paste
1 tsp salt
6 turns black peppermill
450g green beans, trimmed

Heat 6 tablespoons of the olive oil in a pan over a medium heat, add the onion and cook until soft. Add the garlic, tomatoes and tomato paste, salt and pepper, and cook for 2 minutes.

Add the green beans with just enough water to cover them. Put a lid on the pan and bring to the boil, then turn down to a simmer and stew the beans for about 45 minutes. Take the lid off the pan and cook for a further 15–20 minutes to allow the juices to thicken. Stir in the remaining 2 tablespoons of olive oil, and serve.

MUJADARA

I was in two minds whether to make this a main recipe or an accompaniment in the back, but it is so good it deserves to be a recipe in its own right. I would be quite happy with this with a salad for a light lunch. It is the combination of rice, green lentils and crispy fried onions on top that is so successful. Don't throw away the oil from frying the onions. Crisp fried onions are worth sprinkling on a lot of vegetable dishes.

SERVES FOUR TO SIX

200g green lentils, rinsed
250ml sunflower oil
2 large onions, halved
    and finely sliced
2 tbsp olive oil
200g basmati rice, rinsed
¼ tsp turmeric
1 ½ tsp ground cumin
1 tsp ground allspice
400ml *Vegetable stock*
    (page 307) or water
1 tsp salt
12 turns black peppermill
Small handful mint, chopped

Put the lentils in a saucepan, cover with water, bring up to the boil and cook over a medium heat until almost tender, 10–12 minutes. Drain.

In a frying pan over a medium-high heat, warm the sunflower oil. When hot, add a third of the sliced onions, cook until brown and crispy, remove with a slotted spoon to a plate lined with kitchen paper, and repeat with the remaining onions in 2 batches. Set aside.

Wipe out the frying pan. Add the olive oil and heat it, then stir in the basmati rice and the spices and fry gently for 1–2 minutes. Add the lentils and stock or water, bring to a simmer and cook for about 15 minutes, until nearly all the liquid is absorbed. Turn off the heat, cover with a lid and let it rest for 5 minutes. Season with the salt and pepper. Stir in half the fried onions and the chopped mint, and top with the remaining onions to serve.

FREEKEH SALAD

Freekeh is dried green wheat, harvested while the grains are still soft, then sun-dried. It is very common in the Middle East and North Africa, and is used in the same way as bulgur, couscous or pearled spelt. It works well as an accompanying pilaf or a salad, in this case with pomegranate seeds, pistachios, mint and spring onion. *Recipe photograph overleaf*

SERVES FOUR TO SIX

200g freekeh, pearled
   spelt or pearled barley
1 litre water
Salt and freshly ground
   black pepper
5 tbsp olive oil
4 spring onions,
   finely chopped
Seeds 1 pomegranate
Handful flat-leaf parsley,
   roughly chopped
Handful mint,
   roughly chopped
1½ tbsp pomegranate
   molasses
2 tbsp pistachios,
   roughly crushed

Put the freekeh and water in a pan together with 1 teaspoon of salt and 1 tablespoon of the olive oil, bring to the boil, then turn down to a simmer and cook for 15 minutes until just tender. Drain and allow to cool.

When cool, mix together the freekeh with the spring onions, pomegranate seeds and herbs, and season with salt and pepper. Whisk together the remaining 4 tablespoons of olive oil and the pomegranate molasses with a pinch of salt, and dress the salad with it, mixing gently. Serve topped with pistachios.

TURKISH SPICED PILAF

I would say this is almost the bread and butter of Turkish pilafs. It has everything you might expect, namely cinnamon, pine nuts and currants. It was made for me by the owner of a restaurant in Alaçatı, near İzmir, who also made the lamb tandir on page 144, which was gloriously moist and falling apart. They went perfectly together.

SERVES FOUR

300g basmati or
  long-grain rice, rinsed
2 tbsp olive oil
1 onion, halved and sliced
½ tsp ground cinnamon
½ tsp salt
6 turns black peppermill
450ml water
Small handful flat-leaf
  parsley, chopped
Small handful dill, chopped
2 tbsp pine nuts
2 tbsp currants

Soak the rice in plenty of cold water for 30 minutes, then drain.

In a saucepan with a lid, heat the olive oil over a medium heat and fry the onion for 3–5 minutes until soft. Add the rice and toast in the oil. Add the ground cinnamon, salt and black pepper and stir in the water. Bring up to the boil, then immediately turn down to a gentle simmer and put the lid on the pan. Cook for 10 minutes or until the water is just absorbed.

Turn off the heat, keep the lid on the pan, and leave to rest for 5 minutes before stirring through the chopped herbs, pine nuts and currants, and serve at once.

TURKISH RICE

For me an unusual dish in that it mixes rice with orzo pasta, which looks like large rice.

1 ½ tbsp butter
6og orzo pasta
200g medium- or long-grain
　rice, rinsed
5ooml water
½ tsp salt

In a saucepan with a lid, heat the butter and lightly brown the orzo, then add the rice and water. Bring up to the boil, then immediately turn down the heat. Add the salt, put the lid on the pan and leave to cook for 10 minutes. Turn the heat off and leave, still covered, for 5 minutes. Serve immediately.

BULGUR PILAF

400g bulgur wheat, rinsed
5og butter
1 green pepper, deseeded
　and chopped
6 spring onions, chopped
½ onion, grated
2 tomatoes, peeled and
　chopped (or 250g
　tinned tomatoes)
5ooml *Chicken stock*
　(page 307), hot
1 tsp salt
6 turns black peppermill

Soak the bulgur wheat in cold water to cover for 10 minutes, then drain.

In a frying pan with a lid, melt the butter, add the drained bulgur wheat and stir to toast for a minute. Add the rest of the ingredients. Put the lid on and simmer for 10 minutes until the stock has been absorbed. Serve at once.

★★★★★★★ DESSERTS

The flavours of rosewater, honey, almonds, walnuts, pistachios, lemons and oranges, filo pastry, almost no cream and butter – there's an Eastern exoticism about the desserts in this chapter.

❦

In the initial stages of preparing this book, I wanted to call it my Byzantine odyssey, but I was concerned this might sound too esoteric. Even so, I have tried to show that much of the cooking of the region is influenced by the thousand-odd years of the Byzantine or Eastern Roman Empire – roughly 330 to 1453 – and nowhere is this more apparent than in the sweets. Byzantine or Ottoman, it's hard to say where one stops and the other starts: the flavours of rose water, honey, almonds, walnuts, cinnamon, pistachios, lemons and oranges, filo pastry, almost no cream and butter – there's an Eastern exoticism about the desserts in this chapter, poised halfway between the flour, cream and eggs of our own lovely puddings and the almost unbearably sweet and perfumed desserts of the Indian subcontinent.

In this part of the world, sweets are something to be enjoyed with a Greek or Turkish coffee in the middle of the afternoon. The spoon sweets of Greece are made simply by macerating and slow cooking grapes, preferably Muscat, in sugar and serving them cold, spooned on to Greek yogurt. They are one of the best and simplest accompaniments to a coffee I have come across, and well suited to serving as a dessert too. Thinking of cakes taken as an accompaniment to coffee in a café, I love the hazelnut halva on page 302 and the syrup-soaked walnut cake, karidopita, on page 288. The recipes in this chapter are not all of Byzantine or Ottoman origin; there are also sweets in Croatia with an Austro-Hungarian influence – the sour cherry strudel and the fresh fig tart come to mind. The beautiful crème caramel flavoured with rosewater, rožata, of Croatia is a perfect example of a dish at the crossroads of East and West.

TIRAMISU

Why, you may ask, include a recipe for tiramisu? It is now as common as apple crumble. But I was particularly taken by this one in Venice, which had elevated the pudding to a fine-dining level simply by putting it in a cocktail glass and using a whisked fatless sponge.

SERVES EIGHT

For the whisked sponge
3 eggs, separated
75g caster sugar
75g plain flour, sifted with
½ tsp baking powder

For the mascarpone cream
6 eggs, separated
6 tbsp icing sugar
600g mascarpone cheese,
    room temperature
1 tsp vanilla extract

To finish
325ml strong espresso,
    at room temperature
45ml Marsala, Madeira
    or sweet sherry
75g dark chocolate
    (70 per cent cocoa
    solids), grated

Heat the oven to 180°C/gas 4. Grease and line an 18cm x 25cm Swiss-roll-type tin.

Make the sponge. In a bowl, whisk the egg whites until stiff but not dry, then set aside. In another bowl, beat together the egg yolks and sugar with an electric whisk until pale and creamy. Add a little of the egg white to loosen the mixture, then fold in a third of the flour, then a third of the egg white. Repeat until all the flour and egg white is incorporated, folding carefully to retain as much air as possible in the egg whites. Pour into the prepared tin and bake for 25 minutes until risen and lightly golden. Leave to cool, then remove from the tin.

To make the mascarpone cream, beat the egg whites in a clean bowl with an electric whisk until stiff but not dry. Set aside. In another bowl, beat the egg yolks with icing sugar until creamy. Add the mascarpone cheese and vanilla and beat until smooth. Loosen the egg yolk mixture with a spoonful of the whites, then fold in the remaining whites, keeping the mixture very light.

Assemble 8 cocktail or wine glasses and put a spoonful of the mascarpone cream into each. Cut the sponge into 16 pieces to fit the glasses. Take 8 pieces, dip in espresso mixed with the Marsala and place one in each glass. Top with more mixture and then add a second piece of soaked sponge. Finish with a layer of mascarpone cream. Smooth over, then cover with cling film.

Cover and refrigerate for a minimum of 6 hours but preferably overnight to allow the mixture to set firm. Sprinkle with grated chocolate just before serving.

CHOCOLATE GELATO WITH ORANGE & HAZELNUT BISCOTTI

The Italians make chocolate ice cream better than anybody because there is no cream in it and the chocolate is of a high cocoa solid content, giving a fresh but slightly bitter taste. Sometimes, with a really good one, I say, 'Is this a sorbet or an ice cream?' The biscotti recipe is Portia Spooner's. She keeps bringing a box down to Padstow and I scold her because I can't resist them.

SERVES FOUR TO SIX

For the biscotti
Zest 1 orange
100g caster sugar
1 egg
120g plain flour, sifted
    with ½ tsp baking
    powder, plus extra
    flour for dusting
100g whole hazelnuts

For the gelato
750ml full-fat milk
120g dark chocolate
    (70 per cent cocoa
    solids), broken
    into pieces
6 egg yolks
125g caster sugar

To make the biscotti, heat the oven to 180°C/gas 4. Line a baking sheet with baking parchment.

In a bowl, whisk together the orange zest, sugar and egg, then mix in the sifted flour and baking powder, and the hazelnuts. You should have a fairly stiff dough. Flour a board and roll the dough into a thick sausage about 30cm long. Put on the lined baking sheet and bake for 30 minutes, then remove from the oven.

When cool enough to handle, cut on the diagonal into 16 slices about 1cm thick and return to the baking sheet. Lower the oven temperature to 160°C/gas 3 and cook the biscotti on one side for 10 minutes, then turn over and cook for a final 10 minutes. Cool on a wire rack. When cold, store in an airtight tin.

For the gelato, bring the milk to a simmer in a pan then remove from the heat. Put the chocolate and about 100ml of the hot milk in a bowl set over a pan of gently simmering water and leave to melt. Then stir into the rest of the milk and set aside.

In a large pan, whisk together the egg yolks and the sugar, then stir in the chocolate milk. Cook over a gentle heat to thicken the custard, but do not allow to boil. When the mixture coats the back of a wooden spoon, set aside to cool. Pour into an ice-cream maker and churn until the ice cream is soft set. Serve with the biscotti.

CROATIAN SOUR CHERRY STRUDEL

I can't get over how good this is. You don't need to bother with fresh cherries; tinned, jarred or even frozen are perfect, particularly the Polish ones that are on sale in jars in supermarkets (and in a very good Polish shop in Bodmin). This is an excellent store-cupboard dish: tinned cherries, walnuts and frozen filo pastry. *Recipe photograph overleaf*

SERVES EIGHT

2 x 600g jars pitted cherries, drained (drained weight about 600g), or 600g frozen cherries
75g golden caster sugar
Zest 1 small lemon
6 sheets filo pastry
60g butter, melted
50g walnuts, ground in a food processor or finely chopped
Icing sugar, to finish
Cream, ice cream or custard, to serve

Heat the oven to 200°C/gas 6. Line a baking sheet with baking parchment.

Drain the cherries very well in a sieve over a bowl. If you like, reserve the juices and reduce them down to make a sauce. Mix the drained cherries with the caster sugar and lemon zest.

On a clean tea towel, layer the filo sheets, brushing all but the last sheet with the melted butter, and leaving enough to brush the top when rolled. Spoon the cherry filling down one narrow side of the prepared filo sheets in a strip about 8–10cm wide (about a third of the width of the sheet), leaving 2cm free at each end. Cover with the ground walnuts. Tuck the ends of the pastry in and then, using the tea towel, roll the strudel up.

Transfer to the lined baking sheet, with the pastry seam underneath. Brush with the last of the butter. Bake for 10 minutes, then reduce the temperature to 180°C/gas 4 and continue to bake for a further 20–30 minutes until crisp and golden. Allow to cool for a few minutes before cutting into 8 slices. Dust with icing sugar.

Serve warm or cold, with cream, ice cream or custard.

ROŽATA

Croatia really does have some nice sweets. This is essentially a crème caramel flavoured with rose water. It's traditional to have an almond in the centre of each set custard.

SERVES SIX

110g granulated sugar
2 tbsp water
6 whole blanched almonds
4 eggs
30g caster sugar
500ml full-fat milk
100ml double cream
Zest 1 orange
1 tbsp rose water

Assemble 6 ramekins or small dishes. Mix the granulated sugar with the water and heat in a heavy-based pan until the sugar has dissolved, then turn up the heat and cook until you have a dark caramel. Pour a little of this into each ramekin and swirl around, working fast before it sets hard. Set a whole blanched almond in the base of each dish.

Mix the eggs and caster sugar in a bowl. Bring the milk and cream to a simmer in a pan then pour on to the egg mixture. Sieve into a clean bowl or large jug and stir in the orange zest and rose water. Pour into the ramekins.

Heat the oven to 150°C/gas 2. Arrange the ramekins in a roasting tin and pour in boiling water to come halfway up the sides. Cook for 40 minutes until set.

Remove the ramekins from the tin and cool on a wire rack, then refrigerate for 3 hours or overnight. Loosen each custard with a knife and turn out on to a deep plate in a pool of its own sauce.

MASCARPONE DESSERT

I can't remember where I had this in Croatia, but it is just the sort of dessert that you can knock up as an afterthought. Served with strawberries here, but delicious with any summer berries, or a compote of dried fruit in the autumn, or simply grated chocolate.

SERVES FOUR

3 eggs, separated
250g mascarpone cheese
60g tbsp caster sugar
1 tsp vanilla extract
1–2 tbsp milk, if needed
1 punnet fresh strawberries,
    hulled and halved

Whisk the egg whites in a clean bowl with an electric whisk until they hold their shape but are not dry.

In another bowl, beat the mascarpone with the electric whisk. Add the sugar, then the egg yolks and vanilla extract, and mix until you have a smooth cream, adding a tablespoon or two of milk if the mixture is very thick.

Add a tablespoon of the egg whites and stir to loosen the mixture, then carefully fold in the rest of the egg whites, keeping the mixture as light and airy as possible.

Spoon into 4 wine or dessert glasses and top with halved strawberries.

DALMATIAN FRESH FIG TART
Dalmatinska kolac od smokvi

This is exactly my kind of pudding, so easy to knock up when the fig season comes around. One of the pleasures for me of living on both sides of the world is that I get two fig seasons. *Recipe photograph overleaf*

SERVES EIGHT

For the pastry
170g plain flour, sifted,
   plus extra for dusting
Pinch salt
100g unsalted butter, cubed
50g caster sugar
1 egg yolk
50ml double cream

For the filling
500g mascarpone cheese
6 tbsp clear honey
6 large, 7 medium
   or 8 small fresh figs,
   stems trimmed, halved

For the pastry, mix the flour, salt and butter until it resembles breadcrumbs, then stir in the sugar. Mix the egg yolk and cream, and add to the flour mixture so that it comes together to form a dough.

On a floured surface, roll out the pastry and use it to line a 26cm, loose-bottomed flan tin. (If too difficult to handle, wrap and chill for 30 minutes in the fridge.) Trim the edges of the pastry, cover with cling film and rest it in the freezer for 30 minutes.

Heat the oven to 180°C/gas 4. Line the pastry with baking parchment, fill with baking beans or rice and bake blind for 10 minutes. Remove the paper and beans and cook for a further 3 minutes. Take out of the oven and lower the temperature to 160°C/gas 3.

Soften the mascarpone with the honey in a small saucepan over a low heat. Pour into the pastry case, then lay the figs on top, cut-side up. Bake for 30 minutes until just starting to turn golden around the edges. To serve, allow to cool to room temperature before removing from the tin and cutting.

WALNUT CAKE
Karidopita

A delightful, syrup-soaked walnut cake, perfect to accompany a coffee or afternoon tea.

SERVES SIXTEEN

4 eggs
170g soft light brown sugar
Zest 1 lemon
60ml full-fat milk
125ml olive oil, plus
   extra for greasing
300g plain flour
1 tsp baking powder
½ tsp bicarbonate of soda
1 tsp ground cinnamon
Pinch ground cloves
60g walnuts, ground
   in a food processor
   or finely chopped

For the syrup
180g golden caster sugar
225ml water
½ cinnamon stick
Juice 1 lemon

For the syrup, dissolve the sugar in the water in a pan, add the cinnamon and boil for 2 minutes. Allow to cool before removing the stick. Add the lemon juice and set aside.

Heat the oven to 160°C/gas 3. Use baking parchment to line the base of a greased 23cm square tin.

In a large bowl, with an electric whisk, mix the eggs with the brown sugar, lemon zest, milk and olive oil. Sift in the flour, baking powder and bicarbonate of soda. Add the spices and walnuts and mix well. Pour into the tin and bake for 35–40 minutes until a skewer comes out clean.

Pierce the cake all over with a skewer and pour the syrup over while the cake is still warm. Allow to cool in the tin. When cool, turn the cake out and cut into diamond-shaped pieces.

GREEK ALMOND COOKIES
Amygdalota

In Monemvasia there is a shop that specializes in these crescent-shaped almond sweets dusted with icing sugar. For the Greeks, you simply can't leave without a box. It's so nice to see that they are still made above the shop, even though so enormously popular. I think what makes them special is the small, subtle amount of rose water.

MAKES ABOUT TWENTY

130g caster sugar
250g ground almonds
1 tbsp rose water
Pinch salt
2 egg whites
2 tbsp icing sugar

Heat the oven to 180°C/gas 4. Line 2 baking sheets with baking parchment.

In a mixing bowl, combine the sugar, ground almonds, rose water and salt. In a separate clean bowl, whisk the egg whites to soft peaks with an electric whisk. Add a tablespoon of the egg whites to the almond mixture to loosen the dough. Fold in the remaining egg whites to form a stiff dough.

With damp hands, mould the mixture into about 20 walnut-sized balls, then roll each into a sausage shape and turn in the edges to create a crescent. Arrange the crescents on the lined baking sheets and bake for 15 minutes until golden. Remove to a wire rack and allow to cool fully, then dredge with the icing sugar. Store in an airtight tin for up to a week.

THREE-MILK CAKE
Trilece

The idea for this recipe comes from a wonderful fish restaurant in Istanbul on the Bosphorus called İsmet Baba. They have some great blue fish dishes, both grilled and fried, but what really stood out for me – weirdly – was this pudding; they told me it was Albanian. Over the period of writing and filming for this book, I have discovered that there is a lot more to Albanian cooking than I once thought, but that more information is available from Albanians living outside their country than inside. This is a case in point, but it is spectacularly good – the lightest of sponges saturated in three different types of milk: regular milk, evaporated milk and double cream. I have been at it again modifying things, however, and the topping that was a caramel is now salted caramel.

SERVES SIXTEEN

For the cake
Vegetable oil, for greasing
6 large eggs, separated
300g caster sugar
400g plain flour, sifted
    with 2 tsp baking powder
2 tsp vanilla extract

For the three-milk soak
1 litre full-fat milk
400ml evaporated milk
400ml double cream

For the salted caramel sauce
450g granulated sugar
120ml water
45g cornflour, slaked
    with 3 tbsp water
240g butter, cubed
½ tsp sea salt flakes

Heat the oven to 180°C/gas 4. Line a shallow roasting tin, about 30cm x 40cm, with baking parchment and grease the sides.

For the cake, beat the egg whites with an electric whisk until starting to hold their shape, then add the sugar a third at a time, whisking until you have a glossy white mass. Add the egg yolks, one at a time, whisking after each addition. Add the sifted flour and baking powder and fold in well with a large spoon or spatula. Stir in the vanilla extract. Spoon into the prepared tin and smooth the top. Bake for 30 minutes until lightly coloured on top and spongy to the touch, slightly shrinking back from the sides of the tin. Turn out on to a wire rack to cool, then peel off the parchment.

Mix the three milks together and pour half into the roasting tin. Return the sponge to the tin, making holes with a fork all over the top, then pour over the remaining milk mixture. Allow the cake to soak up the milk.

Make the caramel by heating the sugar in a heavy-based pan until it melts and starts to brown. Swirl the pan a little and keep an eye on it while it turns to a deep brown caramel colour. When ready, remove from the heat and add the water. Stand back as it will spit alarmingly. Swirl in the pan and return to the heat. Add the slaked cornflour and the butter, and stir until thick enough to coat the sponge. Add a little more water if it seems too thick. Stir in the sea salt flakes, then spread over the cake and leave to cool. Cut into squares to serve.

GALAKTOBOUREKO WITH ORANGE SYRUP

The Greeks love their sweets, and this one is almost as central to their cooking culture as baklava or rice pudding. To make it as light as possible, I whisk the egg yolks and sugar until pale and creamy; I whisk the whites to soft peaks and fold in. It is quite common to add an orange sauce to galaktoboureko. I made this one typically sweet and sticky.

SERVES EIGHT

For the custard pastry
100g unsalted butter,
    melted, plus extra
    for greasing
3 eggs, separated
125g golden caster sugar
½ tsp vanilla extract
90g semolina
1 litre full-fat milk, warmed
7 sheets filo pastry

For the oranges in syrup
3 oranges
440g caster sugar
190ml water
2 tbsp lemon juice

Heat the oven to 180°C/gas 4. Lightly grease a 20cm springform cake tin.

In a large bowl, whisk together the egg yolks, sugar and vanilla extract with an electric whisk until pale and creamy. Gradually beat in the semolina and the warmed milk. Put this mixture into a clean pan and cook over a low heat for up to 10 minutes until thickened, stirring constantly.

In a clean bowl, whisk the egg whites with an electric whisk to stiff but not dry peaks. Loosen the semolina custard with a spoonful of the mixture, then fold in the rest.

Brush each sheet of filo pastry with the melted butter and lay in the springform tin, alternating the direction the excess will drape over the sides (don't trim it off), until you've used 6 sheets. Pour the custard mixture into the pastry-lined tin and fold the overhanging sheets over the top, tucking in the ends. Place the final sheet of filo, buttered and folded in half, on top. Tuck in the sides and butter the top. Bake in the oven for 45–50 minutes until the custard mixture has set. Check after 30 minutes and cover with foil if the top is getting too brown.

Zest the oranges, then peel them and cut the fruit across into thin slices, removing excess pith. Heat the sugar and water in a pan. When the sugar has dissolved, add the orange zest and lemon juice and simmer for 8–10 minutes until you have a thick syrup. Add the orange slices to the syrup, then set aside.

Allow the pie to cool to room temperature before releasing from the tin. Cut into slices with a serrated knife and serve with the oranges in syrup.

GREEK GRAPE SPOON SWEETS WITH LEMON

Spoon sweets are a great tradition in Greece, but I had never come across them before. When I had these with yogurt at the International restaurant in Symi (made from the sticky Muscat grapes I was buying in the shop round the corner), I thought: this is just the sort of pudding I always choose. It is still very nice made with bog-standard red or white grapes from the supermarket, flavoured with lemon or orange.

Recipe photograph overleaf

SERVES EIGHT TO TEN

500g white grapes
(Muscat if possible),
deseeded if required
200g sugar
Juice 2 lemons
Zest ½ lemon
100ml water

To finish
1–2 tbsp warm water
Greek-style yogurt,
or the Turkish dessert
Muhallabia (page 301)

Put all the ingredients into a pan and bring to the boil. Turn down to a simmer and cook for 40–50 minutes until the consistency starts to turn jammy. Take off the heat and loosen with some of the warm water. Serve with yogurt or muhallabia.

TURKISH DELIGHT WITH ROSE PETALS
Lokum

I was a bit worried before watching Turkish Delight being made in Istanbul, as I thought it might be made with gelatine – all those cow's feet! In fact, it is made with cornflour, and always has been. Rose is the traditional flavour. I admit to adding a tiny bit of orange food colouring. In this recipe I use annatto which is natural, but I don't think a drop or two of food dye will do you much harm in a lifetime.

MAKES ABOUT THIRTY-SIX

800g granulated sugar
350ml water
1 tbsp lemon juice
500ml chilled water
125g cornflour
1 tsp cream of tartar
A few drops of annatto
    food colouring (optional)
1 tbsp rose water
1 tbsp food-grade rose petals
Vegetable oil, for greasing

To finish
175g icing sugar, plus
    extra for dusting
40g cornflour

Start by making a syrup. Mix the sugar, water and lemon juice in a pan, heat to dissolve the sugar then boil hard until the temperature reaches 112–116°C on a kitchen thermometer (or until a small amount of syrup dropped into water forms a soft ball). Turn off the heat.

In a separate pan, whisk the chilled water with the cornflour and cream of tartar, making sure there are no lumps. Continue to whisk as you heat the mixture and bring it up to the boil. It will start to thicken alarmingly into a gluey paste. When really thick, remove from the heat.

Gradually add the sugar syrup a little at a time, whisking after each addition. Return this gluey mixture to the heat and bring to the boil, stirring frequently, then simmer the mixture for about an hour. It will turn a lovely amber colour. At this point you can decide whether or not to add food colouring. Add the rose water and rose petals and stir well.

Lightly grease a tin or mould about 22cm square, line with baking parchment and grease again. Spoon the Turkish Delight into the tin and level the top, then allow to cool on a wire rack.

When completely cold, dust a board with icing sugar, loosen the edges of the tin with a knife and turn out the Turkish delight. Using a lightly oiled knife or pizza cutter, cut into strips and then into squares.

Sift the icing sugar and cornflour into a large bowl and add the cubes of Turkish Delight, coat well in the mixture, then store in an airtight tin at room temperature.

MUHALLABIA

This is a very Middle Eastern ground-rice pudding, subtly flavoured with orange flower water and set in a bowl, then served chilled with chopped nuts.

50g ground rice
1½ tbsp cornflour
1 litre full-fat milk
100g caster sugar
75g ground almonds
1½ tbsp orange flower water
2 tbsp chopped pistachios
   or almonds, to serve

Mix together the ground rice and cornflour, then, using a little of the cold milk, blend to a paste with the sugar.

In a pan, heat the rest of the milk and, when almost boiling, whisk in the paste and continue to stir for 10–15 minutes until thickened. Add the ground almonds and continue to stir for a further 5 minutes, then add the orange flower water.

Pour into a glass bowl or individual serving dishes and chill. Decorate with chopped nuts to serve.

HAZELNUT SEMOLINA HALVA
İrmik tatlısı

It never ceases to amaze me how a pudding made by boiling semolina with milk and sugar can become something so exquisite. In this case, it is probably the addition of toasted hazelnuts, vanilla and lemon zest. This is right at the heart of Turkish culture, and is the most perfect sweet to have with a Turkish, Greek or even espresso coffee, which is why the food stylist Aya Nishimura and I decided to cut it into diamond-shaped pieces to sit nicely on a small plate next to a strong coffee.

SERVES TWELVE

500ml full-fat milk
500g granulated sugar
250g semolina
125ml sunflower oil,
    plus extra for greasing
50g whole hazelnuts,
    plus 30g, roughly
    chopped, to serve
Zest 1 lemon
2 tsp vanilla extract

Warm the milk and sugar in a pan over a medium heat and stir until the sugar has dissolved, then turn off the heat.

In a large pan over a medium heat, mix the semolina and sunflower oil and cook for 7–8 minutes, stirring all the time. Add the hazelnuts and lemon zest and cook for a further 7–8 minutes until the semolina is a nice golden brown.

Add the milky syrup a little at a time, stirring until combined. Turn the heat down to very low and continue to cook for about 20–25 minutes, then add the vanilla extract. The semolina mixture by this stage should be holding its shape in the pan when you draw a wooden spoon through it and be quite stiff. Make sure it really is quite firm – 95 per cent of its set is achieved in the pan. The mixture is then turned into a lightly oiled bowl, mould or tin to finish setting.

Serve cool or barely warm. Turn out and sprinkle with the chopped hazelnuts.

PISTACHIO BAKLAVA

Baklava, that fabulous combination of crispy filo pastry, chopped nuts and syrup, was probably developed in the Topkapı Palace kitchens. When you're in Istanbul, look at those kitchens – the chimneys are a work of art.

MAKES ABOUT THIRTY

100g blanched almonds
200g shelled pistachios
60g soft light brown sugar
1 tsp ground cinnamon
A few rasps freshly
    grated nutmeg
Zest ½ lemon
75g butter, melted
8 sheets filo pastry

For the syrup
200g granulated sugar
125ml water
1 tbsp lemon juice

Make the syrup by dissolving the granulated sugar in the water over a medium heat. Once dissolved, bring to the boil and boil for 4–5 minutes until you have a thick syrup, then add the lemon juice. Set aside to cool.

In a food processor, blitz half the almonds and pistachios until finely chopped. Chop the remaining nuts more coarsely. Reserve 1 tablespoon of the coarsely chopped nuts for decoration. Mix the fine and coarsely chopped nuts with the sugar, spices and lemon zest.

Heat the oven to 180°C/gas 4. Using a baking tin about 20cm x 30cm, cut the sheets of filo in half widthways to fit the tin. Lay a sheet of filo in the tin, brush it well with melted butter and top with 3 more sheets, brushing each with butter. Top with a third of the nut mixture. Repeat with another 4 sheets of filo, brushing each layer with butter. Top with another third of the nuts, then another 4 sheets of filo, buttering each time, then the final third of the nuts. Finish with the last 4 sheets of filo, brushing each with butter.

Score the top couple of layers with a sharp knife into about 30 rectangles of 3cm x 5cm. Bake for 30 minutes until golden brown. Once cooked, pour over the cooled syrup. Ideally wait 4 or more hours before serving, cut into pieces and sprinkled with the remaining nuts.

EXTRAS

BYZANTINE SPICE MIX

1 slice nutmeg
Pinch coriander seeds
4 cloves
1cm cinnamon stick
Pinch ground ginger
Seeds 1 green cardamom pod
⅛ tsp turmeric
⅛ tsp chilli powder

Grind with a pestle and mortar
or in an electric grinder. Store
in an airtight tin or box.

RICK'S RED PEPPER PASTE

660g red peppers
50g tomato paste
½ tsp salt
1 tsp cayenne pepper
30ml olive oil

Roast the red peppers for 20–30
minutes at 220°C/gas 7 until dark
and softened. Transfer to a bowl
and cover with cling film, then
leave until cool enough to handle.

Remove the charred skins,
stalks and seeds. In a liquidizer
or using a stick blender, blitz the
red peppers with the remaining
ingredients. Store for up to a
week in a jar in the fridge.

FLATBREAD/ PIZZA DOUGH

*Makes 4 large, 8 small or
60 mini flatbreads/pizzas*

500g strong bread flour
   plus extra for greasing
7g sachet fast-acting yeast
Pinch sugar
10g salt
275ml lukewarm water
60ml olive oil plus extra
   for greasing

Sift the flour into a large bowl
and add the yeast, sugar and salt.
Make a well in the centre and
add the water and olive oil. Bring
together into a rough dough.

Knead on a floured work surface,
or in a food mixer with a dough
hook, for about 10 minutes until
you have a soft, elastic dough.
Place in a clean, lightly oiled
bowl and cover with cling film.
Leave to rise for 30-60 minutes
until doubled in bulk.

Heat the oven to 230°C/gas 8
and heat up baking sheets or
pizza stones.

When ready, divide the
dough into 4, 8 or more pieces.
Roll out with a rolling pin on a
lightly floured surface until you
have rough circles about 3mm
thick (or as described in the recipe).
Bake for 7–10 minutes in batches
if necessary, or until browned in
spots. Serve immediately.

CROSTINI

For crostini, heat the oven to
180°C/gas 4. Cut a baguette into
slices about 6mm thick. Place
in a single layer on a baking tray.
Brush both sides with olive oil,
season with salt and pepper
and bake for 6 minutes on each
side until golden. Store in an
airtight container.

TOMATO SAUCE

Makes about 600ml

6 tbsp olive oil
20g/4 cloves garlic, finely chopped
1kg well-flavoured tomatoes, peeled,
   or 2 x 400g tins tomatoes
Salt and freshly ground black pepper

Heat the olive oil and garlic in
a saucepan. As soon as the garlic
starts to sizzle, add the tomatoes
and simmer for 15–20 minutes,
breaking them up with a wooden
spoon as they cook. Cook until the
sauce has reduced and thickened,
then season with salt and pepper.
The sauce is ready to use. If not
using immediately, leave to cool,
then refrigerate for up to a week
or freeze for later use.

CHICKEN STOCK

Makes about 1.75 litres

Bones from a 1.5kg chicken
   or 450g wings/drumsticks
   or leftover bones from
   a roasted chicken
1 large carrot, roughly chopped
2 celery sticks, roughly chopped
2 leeks, sliced
2 bay leaves
2 sprigs thyme
2.25 litres water

Put all the ingredients in a large
pan and bring to the boil, skimming
any scum from the surface. Leave to
simmer very gently for 2 hours – it
is important not to let it boil as that
forces the fat from the chicken and
makes the stock cloudy. Strain the
stock through a sieve, and simmer
a little longer to concentrate the
flavour if necessary. If not using
immediately, leave to cool, then
chill or freeze for later use.

VEGETABLE STOCK

Makes about 2 litres

2 large onions
2 large carrots
1 celery head
1 bulb fennel
1 bulb garlic
3 bay leaves
1 tsp salt
3 litres water

Slice all the vegetables (you don't
need to peel the garlic), put into
a saucepan with the water, bring
to the boil and simmer for 1 hour.
Strain. If not using immediately,
cool and refrigerate or freeze
for later use.

FISH STOCK

Makes about 1.25 litres

For a richer-flavoured stock,
you could make this with 500g
cheap white fish (such as whiting
or coley) cut into 2cm slices,
instead of bones.

1 onion, chopped
1 bulb fennel, sliced
100g celery, sliced
100g carrots, sliced
25g button mushrooms,
    washed and sliced
Sprig thyme
2.25 litres water
1kg flatfish bones (such as
    brill, sole, plaice) or fillet

Put all the ingredients except
the fish bones into a large pan,
bring to the boil, then turn
down the heat and simmer
gently for 20 minutes. Add
the fish bones (or fish fillet)
and bring back up to a simmer,
skimming off any scum as it
rises to the surface. Simmer
for a further 20 minutes. Strain
through a sieve into a clean
pan and simmer a little longer,
if necessary, until reduced to
about 1.25 litres. If not using
immediately, cool and refrigerate
or freeze for later use.

SHELLFISH REDUCTION
Makes about 250ml

2 tbsp olive oil
3g/1 small clove garlic
250g prawn heads and shells
1 tbsp tomato paste
½ tsp salt
300ml water

Heat the olive oil in a large
pan, then add the garlic and
the prawn heads and shells,
and stir-fry for 2 minutes.
Add the tomato paste, salt
and water. Bring to the boil
and simmer for 10 minutes,
then pass through a sieve,
pushing down on the shells
to extract as much of the prawn
flavour as you can. Discard the
shells. If not using the stock
immediately, cool and refrigerate
or freeze for later use.

GREEK GARLIC & POTATO SAUCE SKORDALIA
Makes about 250g

See page 27 for the almond version.

135g floury main-crop potatoes,
    such as Maris Piper, peeled
½ tsp salt
15g/3 cloves garlic
100ml olive oil
Juice ½ lemon
A little warm water

Cut the potatoes into chunks and
put in a pan of cold salted water
(1 tsp per 600ml). Bring to the boil
and leave to simmer for about 20
minutes until very soft. Drain.
    Put the garlic into a mortar and
pound with ½ teaspoon of salt to a
paste. Add the potatoes and continue
pounding with the pestle until smooth.
Now beat in the olive oil a little at
a time to build up an emulsion.
As with mayonnaise, don't add it
too quickly. Finally, add the lemon
juice, and a little water if necessary
to achieve the right consistency,
which should be like mayonnaise.

HAND-CUT CHIPS FRIED IN OLIVE OIL
Serves 4

The secret to the success of
Greek chips is Greek potatoes
but I make them in summer with
new season Maris Piper potatoes
with good results.

500g Maris Piper potatoes
300ml olive oil
Salt

Peel the potatoes and cut into chips by
hand. They look better if they are not
too uniform. Heat the oil in a frying
pan to 170°C and shallow-fry for about
10 minutes, turning a few times. They
don't need to be covered in olive oil.
Drain, sprinkle with salt and serve.

BRAISED RADICCHIO
Serves 4

Excellent with rich meat
dishes such as the pork in
milk on page 162.

45g butter
1 tbsp olive oil
5g/1 clove garlic, sliced
1 head radicchio, cut
    into 8 wedges, central
    core removed
Salt and freshly ground
    black pepper
Lemon half
100ml chicken or vegetable
    stock (see above)

Melt the butter, add the olive oil
and lightly sweat the garlic. Add
the radicchio wedges and brown
on all sides. Season with salt and
pepper and squeeze over the juice
of half a lemon. Add the stock,
put a lid on the pan and cook
for 2 minutes until wilted.

RADICCHIO & ANCHOVY SALAD
Serves 4–8

10g/2 cloves garlic
4 anchovy fillets
1 tbsp lemon juice
4 tbsp olive oil
½–1 head radicchio

Crush the garlic to a paste
using a pestle and mortar. Add
the anchovies, pound together
with the garlic, then add the
lemon juice and olive oil and
mix well. Shred the radicchio
and dress the salad.

INGREDIENTS

BIGOLI
A thick, solid, spaghetti-like pasta favoured by the Venetians but difficult to source elsewhere. I have substituted bucatini, which is similar but hollow. You could also use regular spaghetti.

CUTTLEFISH INK
Thick black ink is the cuttlefish's defence mechanism, which it shoots out to create a 'smokescreen' in the water and evade its enemy. If you buy cuttlefish whole and are lucky enough, you might find an unbroken silvery sac of ink in the body. Alternatively, some fishmongers sell squid ink in sachets. The sachets have a reasonable fridge life and, if you see them, are worth buying in to make black risotto (page 238) or black pasta.

FREEKEH
Also known as green wheat, this almost grassy-tasting toasted young wheat grain is good in salads. It can also be used in place of bulgur wheat.

GIGANTES
Found throughout Greece, these giant butter beans have a superb taste and texture. If you are lucky enough to live near a Mediterranean shop, you should find them there; they are available online too. Regular butter beans make a decent substitute.

KEFALOTIRI
This hard, salty, ewe's or goat's milk cheese is found throughout Greece and Cyprus and is thought to date back to the Byzantine era. It is used in the Greek mezze dish saganaki and not easy to find, so I have suggested halloumi cheese, with its salty taste and great texture when fried, as a substitute.

MIZITHRA
A Greek ewe's or goat's milk cheese that comes in fresh or aged form. The recipe for petoules (pancakes with grated cheese) calls for the hard, aged variety. A good substitute is the widely available Italian cheese pecorino romano.

ORZO
This is pasta in the shape of large grains of rice, sometimes referred to as rice macaroni. It is used to thicken a stew or sauce or in soups such as pasta e fagioli (page 168) or minestrone. Also served in combination with rice in Turkey. I like to make avgolemono (page 21) with it.

OUZO
The aniseed flavour of this Greek spirit marries beautifully with seafood in the same way that dill does. If not available, try a French pastis instead.

PANKO BREADCRUMBS
Japanese-style breadcrumbs made from crustless white bread that is dried and grated into coarse flakes. They stay crisper than regular breadcrumbs when fried and are useful as a binding ingredient.

POMEGRANATE MOLASSES
This dark tangy syrup is made by reducing pure pomegranate juice. It has a sweet yet almost lemony/tamarind flavour. Very popular in Turkish and Middle Eastern cooking, it is now available in many supermarkets. It keeps well in the store cupboard and can be used in marinades and dressings in place of vinegar and honey.

RED PEPPER FLAKES
In Turkish *pul biber*, and also known in English as Aleppo pepper, dried red pepper flakes are found all over Turkey in markets and street stalls. A staple for many Turkish dishes, they have some heat but not the kick of crushed dried chillies. They can be sourced outside the country from Turkish shops or specialist spice merchants, but because they can be hard to find I have used chilli flakes in these recipes, and in smaller quantities. If you are lucky enough to have red pepper flakes, double the quantity given in this book for chilli flakes.

RED PEPPER PASTE
In Turkish *biber salçası*, sun-dried red pepper paste is widely used in cooking and also as a spread on Turkish bread. It comes in two versions: *acı* or hot and *tatlı* or sweet. The hot version is made with red chilli peppers and the sweet with red bell peppers. I have included a recipe for my own version of the paste on page 307.

SALT COD/STOCKFISH
Both are dried cod: except that salt cod has, as the name suggests, been salted before being dried. Both need long soaking before cooking. Salt cod can be easier to find than stockfish.

TOMATO PASTE
In Turkish *domates salçası* or simply *salça*, this is an intensely flavoured sun-dried tomato paste; you can use Italian tomato paste with a pinch of salt or a little Italian sun-dried tomato paste instead.

WHITE ANCHOVIES
Silvery marinated anchovies, which you can now get in pots at chiller/deli counters, as opposed to their brown, salted cousins that come in tiny tins.

COOK'S TIPS

All teaspoon and tablespoon measurements are level unless otherwise stated and are based on measuring spoons:

1 teaspoon = 5ml
1 tablespoon = 15ml

People in Australia need to make a minor adjustment as their tablespoon measure is 20ml.

It's often useful to be precise with measurements until you get the idea of a dish, then you can always adapt it to suit yourself.

Cooking times are approximate; and see the note about the temperature probe below.

EGGS
Eggs are medium unless otherwise stated. I recommend free-range eggs.

GARLIC
With the arrival of microplanes I don't bother to skin or crush garlic these days. I grate a clove of garlic with the skin on; the garlic grates, the skin doesn't. Weights are given for garlic in this book. If you prefer similar accuracy when using onions, see below.

MEZZE
What makes mezze work is having a number of them: three or four together make a good spread. Pick and choose from different countries if you like.

ONIONS
A rule-of-thumb guide to unpeeled weights:

1 small shallot = 25g
1 small onion = 100g
1 medium onion = 175g
1 large onion = 225g

PRAWNS: DEVEINING
To remove the intestinal tract from prawns (known as deveining), you need a small sharp knife. Run the knife down two-thirds of the length of the prawn shell from the back of the head towards the tail. Using the tip of the knife, hook out the dark-coloured thread – it usually comes out in one piece – and discard. The prawns are now ready for use. I don't bother to do this if there is no gritty, sandy material in the tract, but if you don't like the thought of what the Australians call the 'poo shoot' and want to remove it anyway, I completely understand.

ROASTING PEPPERS
Cut peppers in half lengthways through the stalk. Pull out the stalk and the seeds. Arrange on a baking sheet skin-side up and roast at 220°C/gas 7 for 20 minutes. Transfer to a bowl and cover the top with cling film. When cool, the skins will slip off. I usually roast many more than I need for one recipe and freeze the remainder.

ROASTING PINE NUTS OR FLAKED ALMONDS
Heat a frying pan without oil over a medium heat and add the pine nuts. Cook for a minute or two, shaking the pan every 30 seconds and tossing the pine nuts to prevent them burning. When lightly browned, tip on to a plate to prevent further cooking.

ROASTING WALNUTS
This can be done in the oven at 180°C/gas 4 on a baking sheet without oil. Cook the walnuts for 5–10 minutes until lightly roasted.

TEMPERATURE PROBE
I always use these to get the correct internal temperature of meat, poultry, game and fish. They are cheap and you will get far more accurate results with one of these than by relying on cooking time only. The temperatures below are just before taking off the heat.

Meat, duck, goose and game:
Rare 50°C
Medium rare 55°C
Medium 60°C
Medium–well done 65°C
Well done 70°C

Chicken is ready at 65°C.

Fish ranges from very rare in the centre at 45°C for oily fish such as salmon and tuna, through to moist in the centre at 55°C, to no blood on the bone for a whole fish at 60°C.

Meat and fish continue to cook after being removed from the heat; their temperature will increase by about 6°C. Meat and poultry benefit from resting for 15 minutes after being cooked and before being served.

TOMATOES: PEELING
Traditionally (in this country) tomatoes have been peeled/skinned by blanching in boiling water, refreshing in very cold water and slipping off their skins. I was rather taken with the method used throughout the Eastern Mediterranean. The tomato is held in one hand and a sharp paring knife is used to take off the skin. If particularly skilled, the skin comes off in one long ribbon. This can also be done with old-fashioned potato peelers; the modern swivel-heads ones don't really work.

INDEX

ACKNOWLEDGEMENTS

It's been a joy. Thanks to James Murphy and Alex Smith not only for the brilliant photography and vivid design of the book, but also for great chats in Istanbul about how the book was going to look. Thanks to Mari Roberts, Charlotte Macdonald, Lizzy Gray and Rebecca Smart for commissioning and editing a great book, and for putting up with my slightly less than perfect deadlines. Thanks also to Aya Nishimura, Xenia von Oswald for the beautiful food styling, and Penny Markham for the wonderful props.

I'm so lucky to have such a hard working and sensible home economist in Portia Spooner and, in passing, thanks to chef Alistair Turner for speed testing so many of the recipes and to Viv Taylor, my PA for keeping everything going.

Plenty of gratitude too to the TV crew David Pritchard, Arezoo Farahzad, Chris Topliss, Pete Underwood, Martin Willcocks, and researchers Liz Stone, Anna Maggio, and Fiona Pritchard. Such a pleasure to have been working with most of you for 17 years.

I must thank my wife Sas for organizing so many large dinners in Sydney so I could try out the new recipes, and my stepchildren Zach and Olivia who, I think, had slow cooked lamb four nights running.

Finally this book is in memory of my good friend Alistair McAlpine, who with his Greek wife Athena, one day in the sun in Puglia said: "Why don't you film in Greece and Turkey?"